THE

COMEBACK

A Playbook for Turning Life's Setbacks into Victories

BY
LEIGH STEINBERG

The Comeback:

A Playbook for Turning Life's Setbacks into Victories

Parkland, FL

www.kayppinmedia.com

www.lavettebooks.com

spsales@lavettebooks.com or hello@kayppinmedia.com

Kayppin Media
9924 NW 65 Mnr
Parkland, FL 33076

Lavette Books
5318 Weslayan St.
STE. 154
Houston, Texas 77005

FIRST EDITION

Designed by Germán Blanco

LCCN: 2025950158

ISBN 978-1962447508

Health and Wellness Disclaimer:

This book describes the author's personal experiences and opinions regarding health, wellness, and recovery. It is not intended as medical advice and should not be used to diagnose, treat, cure, or prevent any disease or health condition. Readers should always consult qualified medical professionals before making changes to their health regimen or treatment plan. Neither the author nor the publisher assumes responsibility for any actions taken based on the information presented herein.

Praise For The Comeback

"The Comeback isn't about sports—it's about rebuilding your mindset. Leigh shows how to turn every setback into an opportunity to reinvent yourself and your purpose." **Mark Davis, Managing General Partner Las Vegas Raiders and Owner of the Las Vegas Aces**

"This book is a beautiful reminder that healing and hope go hand in hand. Leigh's honesty and grace show us that redemption is real and that strength begins in the heart." **Randi Mahomes, Philanthropist & Mother of Patrick Mahomes**

"This book is about purpose, not perfection. Leigh shows that even when life tests you, faith, focus, and humility can bring you back stronger. It's a must-read for every competitor." **Steve Young, NFL Hall of Fame Quarterback**

"As a father and coach, I see The Comeback as a guide for life. Leigh shows that true victory isn't about fame—it's about character, humility, and never giving up on yourself." **Galu Tagovailoa, Founder of Raising Champions**

“Leigh’s courage in addressing brain health and player safety helped change the culture of sports. In The Comeback, he proves that integrity and compassion are the real hallmarks of greatness.” **Michael Suk, MD, JD, MPH, MBA, FACS, Orthopedic Surgeon | Physician-Executive | Healthcare Innovator | Founder & CEO, MDEnvoy**

"One important thing football taught me all those years was Perseverance, and Adversity, getting knocked down, and having to get back up. In Leigh's new book, "The Comeback", you'll learn the ultimate of Perseverance and overcoming Adversity!" **Warren Moon, NFL Hall of Fame Quarterback**

“I’ve known Leigh for decades. His story reminds us that leadership isn’t defined by your success—it’s defined by how you rise after loss. The Comeback is the real playbook for life.” **Troy Aikman, Hall of Fame Quarterback & Entrepreneur**

This book is dedicated to

Amy Stoody,

my soulmate and life partner.

Contents

Foreword by Troy Aikman

Leigh Steinberg has been called a lot of things over the course of his career—a super-agent, a power broker, a kingmaker in sports. And while all those titles might be true, to me he's always been something far more meaningful: a friend, a mentor, and one of the most resilient human beings I've ever known.

I first met Leigh when I was just starting out in professional football—a kid with big dreams, a strong arm, and no idea what was waiting on the other side of the draft. From our very first meeting, Leigh stood out. He wasn't just another agent looking to sign an athlete. He was a listener. He wanted to know who I was—not just as a quarterback, but as a person. What did I believe in? What did I care about off the field? What kind of man did I want to be when the cheering stopped?

That was Leigh's gift. He had an incredible ability to see people—not just their stats, their highlight reels, or their endorsement potential, but also their humanity. And for a young athlete navigating the pressures of fame, money, and expectation, that kind of guidance made all the difference. Leigh didn't just represent me; he helped shape me. Over the years, I watched Leigh do the same for countless others—from first-round draft picks to coaches, from movie stars to community leaders. He was more than a negotiator. He was a builder of people. His belief in using sports as a platform for good was ahead of its time. He constantly reminded his clients that our responsibility went beyond touchdowns and trophies. "Make an impact," he would say. "Leave something better than you found it."

That philosophy guided him—and it guided many of us who were lucky enough to call him a friend. But what makes Leigh's story so powerful isn't just the success. It's the struggle. Because like all of us, Leigh's journey took turns he never expected.

There came a time when Leigh, the man who had once represented champions, found himself facing a battle that no one could fight for him. Addiction—that quiet, relentless enemy—crept into his life. It's a word that carries a lot of weight. I've seen it destroy families, derail careers, and take the brightest people to the darkest places. Leigh wasn't immune to it. None of us are. And when the storm hit, it hit hard.

For years, I watched from a distance as he disappeared from the spotlight—the headlines that once celebrated him now chronicled his fall. The man who had once brokered record-breaking deals was suddenly a cautionary tale. But what I remember most about that time wasn't the fall—it was the silence that followed. Leigh wasn't making excuses. He wasn't pointing fingers. He was fighting for his life, one day at a time.

When I saw him again after his recovery, it was clear that something had changed. The sharpness in his mind was still there—the intelligence, the wit, the charisma—but there was also a humility, a depth that only comes from walking through fire and making it out alive. He had been to the bottom, and he'd made the decision that not everyone makes: to climb back up.

That's what this book is about. It's about that climb—not just back to professional relevance, but to personal redemption. Leigh doesn't gloss over the pain. He doesn't skip past the ugly parts. He talks about the park bench, the paper bag, the isolation, the brokenness. But he also talks about faith. About grace. About the people who refused to give up on him, even when he had given up on himself.

And that's what makes his story so powerful. Because the truth is, we all fall. We all fail. We all face moments where we wonder if we've gone too far to ever make it back. But Leigh's story proves that it's never too late to turn it around. His recovery isn't just about getting sober; it's about rediscovering purpose, rebuilding relationships, and committing to helping others find their own way out of the dark.

When Leigh came back, he didn't come back halfway. He rebuilt his business, yes, but more importantly, he rebuilt his life. He became a mentor not just for athletes, but for people from all walks of life. He began speaking openly about addiction, about resilience, about second chances. He used his platform to remind people that the measure of a person isn't how far they fall—it's how they rise afterward. As someone who's spent a lifetime in locker rooms and on fields, I've seen my share of comebacks. I've been part of a few myself. But Leigh's comeback is one of the greatest I've ever witnessed. It didn't happen under stadium lights. There was no roaring crowd, no trophy waiting at the end. It happened quietly, in the day-to-day discipline of choosing life over despair, hope over shame, redemption over regret.

There's a lesson in that for all of us—whether you're an athlete, an executive, a parent, or someone just trying to make it through another day. We all face setbacks. We all have chapters we wish we could rewrite. But what Leigh's journey shows us is that, even when everything falls apart, you can still rebuild—not into who you were, but into someone wiser, stronger, and more compassionate.

When I think about Leigh now, I don't think about the headlines, or the contracts, or the celebrity events. I think about the friend who looked out for me when I was a kid trying to find his footing. I think about the man who turned his pain into purpose. I think about someone who has walked through fire and come out refined—not perfect, but powerful in a whole new way.

This book isn't just a memoir about sports or business. It's a roadmap for redemption. It's about falling hard, standing up slow, and choosing to keep going anyway.

It's a story that says, no matter who you are or where you've been, there's always a way forward.

Leigh, I'm proud of you. I'm proud of the courage it took to write this book—to open up your life, to share your scars, to use your story to help others. That takes a different kind of strength, the kind that doesn't come from power or fame, but from humility, honesty, and heart.

Your journey reminds me—and I think it will remind anyone who reads these pages—that life is about far more than the wins and losses. It's about how you play the game when no one's watching. It's about grace under pressure, faith in the comeback, and the relentless belief that tomorrow can still be better than today.

Thank you for teaching us that redemption is real. Thank you for proving that second chances aren't given, they're earned. And thank you, my friend, for showing us all what it means to never give up on yourself.

— *Troy Aikman*

Acknowledgements

I would like to thank my talented publisher and editor, Lavaille Lavette, for her critical contributions to this book. She is a source of inspiration and has a way of keeping me on track to achieve important things in the world. She has generated projects from Africa to Chicago, all of which enrich people's lives. When writing a book, look no further than Lavaille. I would also like to thank Kayppin Media and Karen Kilpatrick for their belief in this project.

I have dedicated this book to my soulmate, Amy Stoody, who has filled my life with joy and camaraderie. She is my life partner in all affairs. To my kids, too. My son Jon constantly inspires me with his level of achievement in life, as he keeps a bucket list of things to do that expand his experience. And we've welcomed his wonderful wife, Lisa, into our family. And to Matt with his eidetic memory and passion for all things sports and entertainment. My daughter Katie, one of my closest friends and a constant source of joy, is a walking exemplar of remarkable positive energy. To my brothers, Jim and Don, whose contributions to the world I greatly admire and whose loyal friendship I will forever value. To my Aunt Eleanor, our matriarch, a paragon of generosity. My trusty roommate and close friend, Tom Van Voorst, has been an unending source of support and strength, as well. He is a rock. My sponsor, Dwight Heitman, has been a font of central wisdom and support. I absolutely would not have made it this far without his treasured involvement in my life. And my first sponsor, Bill Long, filled my life with laughter and inspiration, while his wife, Nancy, has been a constant source of support.

Much gratitude to Patrick Mahomes, whose gifted achievements on the football field make him the most talented athlete of our generation. His steadfast commitment to faith, family, and giving back to the world continues to make it exciting to work with athletes. To Randi Mahomes, a super mom filled with love and nurturing. And to Patrick Mahomes Sr., I'm so thrilled to be on this journey with you.

To Paxton, Stacey, David, and Evin Lynch for their trust and belief in me, which allowed me to jumpstart my career. To Steve Bartkowski, who had the confidence and belief that I could enhance his life and helped start this journey in 1975. To Ivan Weiss, my initial signee all those years ago.

Thank you to my former client, Nick Lowery, for being an incredible role model, as an athlete and a man. To Steve Young, thank you for the honor of representing you. I am proud of the difference you have made in the world. To Troy Aikman, thank you for the privilege of representing you, and gratitude for always sticking with me.

The highlight of my career has been the long journey I took with my client, and one of my closest friends, Warren Moon. He displayed incredible courage and breakthrough status on the field and is a great role model today. And I cannot imagine a more inspirational figure in my long career than Rolf Benirschke. He's a great friend and terrific role model.

To Garrett and Gale Gilbert, who helped me get started on my return. To Earl Campbell, a gifted friend and inspiration. And to June Jones, one of my closest friends who has been with me every step of the way over the last fifty years. And to every athlete I have represented: thank you for letting me be on this journey with you. Thank you to Jack Friedman, with whom I shared a dorm floor at Berkeley in the sixties and who has remained a best friend all these years. To Scott and Marilyn Irwin for being like a second family to me and helping me resurrect my career. To Gale and Trisha Oliver, steadfast supporters in a critical time. To Julie Stagner for being a vital part of our rebuild. To Fred Edelstein, my longtime friend. In loving memory of Mike Shatzkin, whom I met in speech class at UCLA in 1967 and who stood by me through thick and thin. To Don Peters, who was there when it counted. To Ron Burkle, a superb businessman, philanthropist, and mentor of mine. To my longtime partner, Jeff Moorad, who has stuck with me throughout. Mark Francis, a professor in sports studies, has been a loyal and trusted friend.

To David Blanchard, for helping me restart my business. To Sean Reyes, who structured and papered the comeback. To Scott Bodgan, thank you for your friendship in the rough days. To Eric

Yaverbaum, a genius in all things public relations, you have added so much to my life. Bill Walsh, an incredible serial entrepreneur, has been a great partner on multiple exciting projects. Thank you to Erwin Chemerinsky, the Dean of the University of California, Berkeley Law School, who constantly fights for justice and is a shining beacon of legal excellence.

Many thanks to the gifted event planner Jessica Whitney, whose creativity and excellence bring our Super Bowl Party to life. Thank you to my wonderful friend and trainer, Tony Lattimore, who makes staying in shape a whole lot of fun. We laugh more than we work out. My health, wellness, and athletic performance project has received essential support from Dr. Daniel Amen, Dr. Phillip Yoo, Dr. Greg Vigoren, Dr. Tommy Shavers, Dr. Michael Chan, Dr. Adam Sewell, John Parks, Mark Westaway, and Rowena Gates. To Dr. Jason Keifer, his wife Nicole, and their kids Koji, Elle, Nicson, and Cole, who not only treated my brain but also invited me into their loving family.

Thank you to Dr. Nicole Fisher, my partner in bringing awareness and a solution to the ongoing concussion crisis. Thank you to Dr. Kristen Willeumier, my surrogate sister, for her expertise in brain health and wonderful support when I needed it most. Kevin Yarter, who ran our sober living house, launched this recovery journey with a solid foundation. And to my fellow travelers on this incredible journey: Red Benson, Kent Benson, Ray O'Grady, Ernie Grimm, Jason Massie, Adam Copenhaver, Greg Ellis, Tom Lewdowski, Chip Gendreau, Marlys Goseco, Mike Sansovich, Terri West, Meredith Roundtree, Mike Hanrahan, Larry Webb, J.

D. Denham, Zach Martin, Vincent Ritschel, and Raul Vera, thank you for your friendship. To my home group, thank you for keeping me on the straight and narrow.

Thank you to all my staffers and interns who have been with me along the way. Thank you to my former director of operations, Alex Layton, for his stalwart service. Thank you to Christopher Miles, our current director of operations, who keeps things humming. Thank you to Makena Dunn, my ever-positive right-hand woman, who makes every day better and has been an integral part of this project. To the fans, commentators, broadcasters, those who loved me, and those who criticized me—thank you all. Your support and criticism have inspired and motivated me to improve, do better, and cherish the life I've always dreamed of. This is my life.

Chapter 1

Rock Bottom

Sitting on my deceased father's bed in my family home, mired in a deep depression, I took stock of my life, which was in a state of upheaval. I had closed my office and my business. I had moved out of my condominium. I was alienated from one of my sons. And in the midst of this crash, I had only one thought, one impulse: where can I find more vodka?

Alcoholism had brought me to this point. Many people start a reckless relationship with alcohol as young adults, but I didn't drink in my teen years. My parents never brought alcohol into our house simply because neither of them drank. In college, I was nicknamed "One Beer Steinberg" because that was usually my limit —a moniker that stuck with me for decades. It wasn't until I approached my fifties that things started to change. For most of my adult life, I'd indulge periodically, but never to excess. But in the last few years, I had acquired an uncontrollable drinking habit. I was an addict. And it was destroying my life.

It had started innocently enough, around 2006. Friction in my marriage led me to have a couple of drinks at night, just to take the edge off. No matter how discreet I was about it, though, when you live with people, it's hard to hide the smell of vodka on your breath. But when my ex-wife and I finally separated, I was on my own for the first time in decades, so there was no one to witness my bad behavior or dissuade me from buying liquor. And I was feeling down from the separation and from not seeing my kids every day, which only intensified the need to numb the pain.

Before I knew it, the habit grew into a problem, the problem grew into an addiction, and the addiction overtook me. Within three years, I had become a full-blown alcoholic. It was grim. When I was low on cash, I'd scrounge around for loose change and walk to the liquor store to buy the cheapest vodka available. When I didn't have the money, I became creative. If I were a regular at a store, I would pick up a bottle of vodka and drop it on the counter.

"Hey! You know me, I come here all the time!" I'd greet the clerk. "I just left my wallet back at my house—let me take this bottle and I'll come back and pay you. You know I'm good for it!"

Few people possess the ingenuity of an addict in need of a fix. My creativity and relationship-building skills allowed me to walk out with a complimentary bottle of vodka. I used my charm as a weapon. And then I went up the street to the park and swilled it straight from the brown bag. This was what I had become.

Every addict has a moment when they hit rock bottom, that awful nadir when, just when you think things can't get any worse, they do. Mine came in 2010, when I had to move into my childhood home with my mother, who was in poor health after suffering a stroke years before. Drinking had made it impossible to run my business and operate as a sports agent. It had degraded my relationship with my family and also landed me in legal trouble.

Over the course of just five years, I was arrested for a DUI in 2007, had a public intoxication arrest in 2008, and went bankrupt. Even though my business partner Jeff Moorad and I had split $130 million, the challenging combination of divorce, bad investments, poor luck, and mounting business expenses left me broke. It got to the point where it was hard to afford a meal. My life was an unrecognizable chaotic mess and, even with the growing list of adversities on my shoulders, my only coherent thought was: how can I get more vodka? Rather than plotting my own rescue mission, I was digging myself deeper and deeper into a hole I thought I'd never escape. I felt broken.

My inability to break denial was blocking my voice from uttering a single word for help. I knew I needed help, but vodka dominated my life. The vodka never judged me or spoke back to me, telling me to stop, so I embraced it. With each newly opened bottle came the same empty promise: this is the last one. When the last shot pooled in the bottom of the glass, I told myself: this is the last sip. After work, I would sit in my car in front of my condo vowing not to drink that night. I was committed to having a sober evening.

Yet somehow, magically, my car would drive itself to the nearest gas station and, before I knew it, I was back home, drunk in my apartment. Alcoholism is not just a bad habit or lack of willpower;

it's a disease. It affects the brain. It is chronic and progressive. But to non-alcoholics, watching an alcoholic decline makes it seem as though the alcoholic simply does not have the willpower to stop. They are intentionally choosing bad behavior.

This was deeply frustrating to me. I had willpower. It took extraordinary willpower to build our sports empire. I had done positive things, yet I lost it with my addiction and became helpless. Alcohol had me in its grip.

Cravings for alcohol arise from changes in the brain's reward system and stress circuits, particularly involving the amygdala and nucleus accumbens. At the same time, the prefrontal cortex, responsible for rational judgment, loses regulatory control. Alcoholism directly affects many brain areas, including the frontal lobes, the cerebellum, and the limbic system. Among these regions, the amygdala plays a central role in shaping the powerful emotional pull of alcohol.

The amygdala is part of the brain's emotional and survival circuitry. It helps tag experiences with emotional weight, especially those linked to reward or threat. In alcohol use disorder, the amygdala becomes hypersensitive to alcohol-related cues and memories. This can trigger cravings so powerful that they override the prefrontal cortex, the part of the brain that governs judgment, self-control, and decision-making, making the urge to drink feel as urgent as eating when you're starving or gasping for air when you can't breathe. The amygdala is just one of the many parts of the brain affected by alcoholism. Which is why if you ask an alcoholic,

"Why in the face of all the negative consequences do you continue to drink?" the alcoholic will respond, "I don't know."

We all experience crises in life, when things do not go as planned and everything falls apart. Sooner or later, we reach a low point. Our business or career implodes. We suffer relationship problems with family, friends, and those who love us. We grapple with despondency, despair, or mental illness. We face a setback in our physical health. And in some cases, as with me, all these crises happen at the same time. Thank you to alcohol.

Whatever the cause, we will all, at some point, face major problems that leave us uncertain how to move forward and questioning whether we'll ever be whole again. How does one recover? How does one make a comeback against all odds? Lying on my father's bed, I recalled his steadfast love, his strength of spirit, and his strong moral character. He had raised me right. Where had I gone wrong? What was I doing? Who had I become?

His bedroom was a testament to a life lived in service of others, decorated with plaques and photographs recognizing the charitable and social work he did. Books lined the shelves, written by the great visionaries and civil rights leaders he looked up to. And in a frame hung this quotation: "With all of our troubles, great and small, the greatest are those that never happened at all." It was a sentiment I often thought about during my comeback journey.

I was gazing at the accolades of a great man through the miasma of my own confusion and misery, as the voice inside my head clamored relentlessly, Go get more vodka! When are you going to get more vodka!?

I asked myself, Is this who you want to be? At that point, I had my epiphany. I realized I no longer wanted to be an alcoholic, hiding away my pain with a drink. I knew that, to be the authentic person I wanted to be again, I had to be accountable for who I had become and the destruction I had caused along the way. Yet even among the detritus and wreckage of the relationships, health, and career that the drink had overtaken, I clung to hope. Somehow, some way, I had to pick myself up. I had to try again.

My epiphany gave me the strength to confront these cravings. It was one of both the greatest and worst moments of my life. I understood what I needed to do to kick my addiction, but I also recognized the hurt and pain I had caused many of my family and friends. Thinking about them only increased my desire and focus on changing my life. The last thing I wanted was to be remembered as the alcoholic who lost everything, including the people who loved him.

I needed to do what I hadn't allowed myself to do when my father passed a few years back. Rather than shifting through the moment and ignoring the pain, I had to sit with my grief and accept responsibility for moving forward. Only when I self-reflected about the reality of my situation and assessed my actions could I take the next step.

This is a story about how alcohol abuse nearly destroyed me, ruined my relationships, mauled my emotional health, and sent me down into a dark spiral of helplessness and hopelessness. It is also a story of how I found the road to recovery. How I restored my family relationships, how I reestablished my sports business, and how

I have used this experience to help others who are suffering. My story is a primer on how to bounce back—a showcase of resilience that I hope inspires you.

Vodka was my albatross. Perhaps yours is something else. I'm writing this book for anyone who is struggling or finds themselves going through a dark night of the soul, where they've lost their way and know they need to change course. Based around nine pillars, these are universal principles for anyone seeking to make a comeback. It's how I was able to pull back from the brink, and I am confident they can have the same power in your life. Perhaps this book will spark an epiphany of your own.

Chapter 2

Roots

What was most poignant about that epiphanous moment in my father's room was the vast gulf between how I was raised and who I had become. It wasn't simply that I had lost control of myself to alcohol. It was that I had, in the process, forsaken the values I grew up with, the ones my mother and father had embodied every day of their lives.

For some alcoholics, the root of the problem may start with their upbringing (nurture) or family history (nature). Being exposed to alcohol abuse at a young age can normalize reckless drinking, and there is a clear genetic component to alcoholism.

But genes are not destiny, and many alcoholics cannot point to their origins as the source of their addiction. I'm a living example of that. My family was solid and tight-knit. People know me as Leigh Steinberg, the famous sports agent, the inspiration for the blockbuster film Jerry Maguire, the guy hobnobbing with the likes of Patrick Mahomes and Steve Young, assuming that I've always been a high-flyer who grew up rich. But my origins are humble.

My family of five packed into a small house my parents purchased for $12,000 in the Culver City suburb of Los Angeles. We shared one bathroom for the five of us. My two brothers and I shared a bedroom. My father was a schoolteacher who had to work three jobs to make ends meet. At the beginning of each school year, my father bought five shirts and five pairs of pants for us kids, and we had better like the clothes we picked, because that's all we got! When our jeans got worn out, we patched them. We had tape on the soles of our shoes to preserve them. We collected empty bottles and grease to make soap for sale.

Despite our lack of financial abundance, Mom and Dad kept our household together and imparted strong values on my siblings and me—the kind that would let us thrive later in life.

We were taught the importance of conflict resolution and how to work through disagreements civilly. My father advised us on the best way to communicate. He taught me the art of problem-solving. When I had trouble making the sound "th..." and it came out more like "da" instead of "the," my father made me repeat the following tongue twister: "Theophilus Thadeus Thistledown, the successful thistle sifter, while sifting a sieve-full of un-sifted thistles, thrust three thousand thistles through the thick of his thumb." After repeating this phrase endlessly, I was able to say a clean "th..." This tutelage helped me become a better communicator.

In the Steinberg household, there was an atmosphere of tolerance, responsibility, accountability, and progressive thinking. These foundational rules fueled my parents' zest for living. It was also the glue that kept us all grounded in our purpose as a family and in how best to support our community. Our Jewish faith also imparted values. Among them, the need to make positive contributions to society and be our brother's keeper.

My elementary school, ironically named Stoner Avenue, was directly across the street from a federal housing project. Only families below the poverty line could live there. Its residents were primarily Black and Latino families. So, I grew up in an interracial melting pot. That stayed with me for life. It's why I value diversity and why I fight hard for the underprivileged and those who are discriminated against. From a young age, I learned that the world isn't equal, and some people have an advantage over others. But at least in the bubble of our childhood neighborhood, we were all running around on an even playing field.

When you grow up having sleepovers with friends from different backgrounds, you realize we are all just people. In the adult world, race might matter; it might separate people into haves and have-nots by virtue of skin color. But in the neighborhood, we were simply kids having fun. As kids, we never identified one another by color or ethnicity but as equals who looked out for one another. By no means was my community perfect, but we understood the importance of treating each other equally and with kindness. Growing up in a diverse environment while living in close quarters with my family only reinforced my dad's teachings.

Because of my childhood experiences, I learned how to connect with and relate to others from various backgrounds. It is a tool that has served me well as I succeeded as a sports agent. Accountability was also highly valued in our household. My parents instilled the necessity of a sincere apology when one had erred. "Run down the block and tell him you’re sorry!" my dad would say if I had offended someone. His wisdom still rings in my ear. The key was and is to be honest.

If I spilled the milk and admitted to it, then I would receive a mild admonition to be more careful. If I lied about spilling the milk ... I was in big trouble. We were encouraged to make a daily inventory of those we wronged and to keep track of the apologies we owed. We didn’t go to bed without resolving family conflicts. I still live by that rule today. Going to bed with issues unresolved and waking up the next morning as if everything is normal only comes with a sleepless night and a continuous problem.

When I was a kid, my parents founded the “Muttonhead Club,” a special organization within our immediate family that let us put these values into practice. Using Robert's Rules of Order to conduct our meetings, we selected a President, Vice President, Treasurer, and Sergeant-at-Arms. Here, we discussed new and old business, as well as family issues. I must say that the best part of it all for me was the dessert that followed our meeting. I was able to spend time with my family doing a joint activity that was not just educational at the time but also instilled moral values that we would go on to live by for the rest of our lives.

When we weren’t tackling a problem in the Muttonhead Club, we were making sure we kept each other laughing. Laughter was the soundtrack of our lives and an antidote to day-to-day issues that could, at times, feel overwhelming. I also had a pretty sharp sense of humor and loved the humor of the people around me. Growing up, my friends always competed to see whose silly remarks could be the first to make me spit up any soft drink I was drinking.

I went to high school at Alexander Hamilton High School in West Los Angeles. It was filled with brilliant hyper-competitive students. The toughest academic challenges I faced, including undergrad and law school, were with the incredible students at Hamilton High. My parents raised me to try and make a positive difference in the world, so I gravitated toward politics and was elected Student Body President. I later served as Student Body President at UC Berkeley and then as Class President at UC Berkeley School of Law.

When I continued my education at UCLA in the sixties, I was excited to live my college dream. I joined the fraternity Pi Lambda Phi, followed the national champion UCLA basketball team, shared a class with Kareem Abdul-Jabbar, and made lifelong friends. But the decade was a time of social disruption, so I began a balancing act between pursuing an authentic college education and staying involved with the world around me. So, Berkley beckoned. It was the center of cutting-edge trends and counterculture for the whole country.

Walking down Telegraph Avenue in Berkeley with the Beatles and Jimi Hendrix coming out of every apartment and dorm was a heady experience. Little did I know that Jimi Hendrix and Jim Morrison would later ask me to give them a tour of the campus and the city. Campuses were a cauldron of change and the center of conflict for the larger community. Rock music, new hairstyles, new philosophies, and resistance to the war in Vietnam dominated our lives.

It was a time of fierce idealism and a desire for sweeping reform, tempered by the disillusionment at seeing great leaders and champions of justice, like President Kennedy, Martin Luther King Jr., Malcolm X, and Robert

Kennedy, gunned down. The cultural and political upheaval, and the generational conflict between the old guard and the young Baby Boomers clamoring for change, penetrated our lives. My education took place through student activities almost as much as in the classroom.

In 1967, President Lyndon B. Johnson came to California to fundraise. Outside of the Century Plaza Hotel, where he stayed, a group of us gathered alongside my hero, heavyweight champion Muhammad Ali, to protest the Vietnam War. My father had always taught us the importance of standing up for those who couldn't speak for themselves. Ali embodied this ideal, too—he put a lot on the line in his advocacy for civil rights and opposition to the Vietnam War, and he paid a price. I, too, believed the war was a colossal, tragic waste of American and Vietnamese lives; so, it was my duty to oppose it, even as I sympathized with and admired the troops for their bravery and respected the suffering they endured for being made to fight an unwinnable war.

That day outside the hotel, the protest was planned to be peaceful. Many had gathered to hear Ali give a speech at the rally at Rancho Park. But everything went awry when the police decided to make a move on the crowd. Suddenly, they charged our peaceful protest with batons and weapons.

I left the protest entirely in shock. Most of the people there were my peers, fellow students who were asserting our independence as young adults and exercising our right to protest, but we were attacked by the same officers who had taken a sworn oath to protect us. I couldn't find a plausible reason for their actions.

Although I still held the utmost respect for the police in general, it made me question the institution, and it gave me a deeper understanding of how Black Americans experience police in the inner city. I saw what consequences confrontations with the police could bring. I saw the dangers that could come from violence in the streets. I still thought protests were necessary, but there needed to be a better model for conflict resolution. Settling issues in boardrooms rather than on the street was a vital step. It was that same strength of standing up for my beliefs that motivated me when I hit bottom.

Though I was disillusioned and destabilized after protesting, I still wanted to stand up and fight. It was time to sit by myself and figure out my priorities, and this could only happen via self-reflection. In the midst of campus unrest, I ran for and won the election for Student Body President. At the time, the governor of California was Ronald Reagan, who also served on the Board of Regents governing the UC campuses. Governor Reagan sought to crack down on the campuses and quell the rampant student unrest. The more we demonstrated, the more he reacted with fury.

In 1970, the US bombing and incursion into Cambodia inflamed a wave of furious protests coast to coast, and at Berkley and other UC campuses, students objected passionately. Reagan was furious. He wanted to fire the chancellor of Berkeley, Roger W. Heyns, presumably because he wasn't cracking down hard enough on student unrest. I went in front of Governor Reagan to defend the Chancellor at a Regents meeting. He stared across a table at me and asked, "Weren't you the same Mr. Steinberg who was arrested blocking troop trains in Oakland in 1960?"

"Well, Governor," I said, "I was, like, ten years old in 1960. If I was doing anything with trains, it would have been playing with toy trains, not sitting in front of troop trains." Over the years, I improved my communication with the governor and, when he became President, he gave me a Humanitarian Award, and we laughed about the good old days.

When my father decided to forgo the family business—restaurants and nightclubs—to become a teacher, his father—my grandfather—was confused and disappointed. My grandfather, John, ran Hillcrest Country Club, which was a hangout spot for many movie stars. So, I had the conflicting influence growing up of a father who cared about education and a grandfather deeply ensconced in the entertainment industry. My grandfather played Gin Rummy every day with comedians Jack Benny, George Burns, Groucho Marx, Danny Kaye, and George Jessel. He took me to my first baseball game, which was with the Hollywood Stars of the old Pacific Conference League.

I took a picture on the lap of superstar actress and cultural icon Marilyn Monroe. My grandfather had made plans for my future career. His connections would help him find me work as an actor. He fantasized about making me the next Gregory Peck. So rightfully so, in my grandfather's eyes, why would my dad accept lower pay to work in a teaching position? As opposed to the world of glamor my grandfather lived in. My dad invited him to come and see the school, thinking that if he stepped into the environment, he might understand.

Reluctantly, my grandfather finally decided to visit, and his heart softened. He watched as my father taught with a gentleness that only a parent could provide. My grandfather watched the glow on the students' faces and saw how they responded to my father. When the school day came to a close and the children had left the classroom to return home, my grandfather looked at my dad and sighed.

"I get it now, son," he said.

My father went on to become a vice principal and later principal at schools like La Conte Junior High and Fairfax High School, but his other passion was human relations and fighting bigotry. He wrote his doctoral thesis on education and human relations. And he served for thirty years on the Los Angeles Commission on Human Relations; he was its president for several of those years.

To say I had the best dad in the world would be a gross understatement. He was the most authentic person I have ever known. I loved the way he kept his life together and kept us together as a family. I was also constantly inspired by his emphasis on morality and ethics. My mother, Betty, was a font of enthusiasm and energy with a wicked sense of humor. She instilled in me a love of books, movies, and the beach, and inspired me to fight for social justice. My mother was a librarian who pioneered the concept of public libraries being used to check out films, and later DVDs. Together, you could feel their love from a mile away. My dad and mom were great mentors to me and to my children. It took me some time to truly remember my father's admonitions, but I've always had the drive never to give up and always to try to find the light at the end of the tunnel, even if I couldn't see it just yet. Nobody in our household was raised as a quitter.

Yet I wanted to be so much like my father and have that positive outlook. I just didn't have a real starting point once the addiction took over. I reminisce about these early days because they helped shape the man I am, even decades later. They gave me a foundation. All comebacks have an external and internal element. But intertwined with the outer journey is an inner journey, a battle of character. Almost all the pillars of a comeback I discuss in this book come from within. And that starts with connecting with the essential moral values that make you who you are. These are probably the values you grew up with.

Maybe they're values you cultivated as you ventured out into the world. But if you've lost your way, go back to the path you knew before it all fell to pieces. That's how you start again.

Chapter 3

Patience: Don't Jump the Snap

Football is a game of timing. Expediency is often rewarded, but hasty decisions will work against you. A quarterback who forces a throw into double coverage risks an interception. A defensive lineman who jumps a half-second early gives the opponent five free yards. Even in free agency or contract negotiations, impatience can cost a career opportunity. In this business, patience and discipline are the difference between winning and losing.

The same applies off the field. When an athlete's career, health, or personal life is unraveling, there's no quick fix. You can't just call the right audible and change everything overnight. It's more like trying to rebuild a struggling franchise—you may have talent, but if the playbook is flawed, the locker room culture is broken, and the leadership has lost its way, turning it around will take time. That's the situation I faced. My descent didn't happen in a single play; it was a slow, grinding drive in the wrong direction.

By the time I realized it, I had lost far more than a game; I had wrecked my life. Just as it takes years to rebuild a team into a contender, it was inevitable that it would take at least as long to reverse the damage in my own life. This chapter is about patience: the acceptance that change rarely happens overnight, that bouncing back is a long-term project involving many fits and starts. Two steps forward, one step back. A long road.

At sixty-one, I was a functioning alcoholic. I'd drink my way through the night and still arrive at the office on time. Because my sports agency was still flourishing, I'd tricked myself into believing I'd mastered the balancing act between productivity and alcoholism. In a nutshell, I had mastered nothing and only sank deeper into my addiction. What I thought was hidden, everyone in the office saw. Even though I was the boss, the people working for me were not afraid to confront me about it.

They did not want me driving around drunk. To their credit, my staff was aware that I was struggling and took steps to prevent negative consequences from occurring by holding episodic interventions and private one-on-one talks with me. They even came to my apartment, grabbed my wallet and keys, and pushed me to go and stay in rehab to solve the problem. People like Warren Moon confronted me and said, "I know you're struggling and, until you stop, I want to make sure nothing tragic happens to you."

I accepted what Warren had to say, though I fluctuated between denial and openness and acceptance. I was often tempted to tell the individuals trying to help me that they were wrong and that I had it under control. But deep down, even I knew that was a lie.

Alcoholism is a disease that tells you that you don't have a disease and that the problem is the people telling you that you have a problem. Part of it is profound denial. Alcoholism is a clever and sneaky disease that plays many tricks with your mind.

During your struggles, your ups and downs, people close to you may confront you about your behavior. Instead of rejecting these observations, one needs to be open to their perspective and advice. Try not to be defensive or show contempt before investigating and rejecting their advice. There is a very good chance you will not like the truths presented, but remember, they are for your own good. When I started listening to those around me and doing an internal inventory, I began to break denial.

Take responsibility for your situation, let go of any guilty feelings, and don't let the shame you may have hold you back from getting the help you need. Admitting you have a problem is the beginning of working on a solution. When I struggled to face my addiction, isolation was my friend. I mostly drank late at night by myself in my condominium. Though it was never my intention, I can definitely see how my actions of separation and seclusion would appear to the naked eye. The reality was that I was just hiding my dark secret. A lot of things were happening in my family's life during my addiction that I totally missed. If I could have those six or seven years back to do impactful things, it would be a blessing.

I prided myself on the false belief that nothing could throw me off my game, both professionally and personally. There will always be ebbs and flows in business, after all. I was at peace with the idea that we would sign some great clients and others would say no. I knew that, notwithstanding our best efforts at planning, some projects would go awry. I understood that outside developments could frustrate our best business plans. But I didn't feel the overwhelming need to win every battle that landed in my lap. I knew I could use my collective skills to make the best of any circumstance.

When I was in this dark place in my life, I thought I could make it to a brighter tomorrow, just like Steve Young, the former San Francisco 49ers Hall of Fame quarterback. When I sat with Steve and asked him what he was most excited about, his answer was being able to use his skill set to succeed. So the irony of the story you are about to read is that someone whose highest goal was to be at the center of play on a football field was continually frustrated in his search for a starting role. Clearly, Steve Young's comeback was being named the starting quarterback of the 49ers.

STEVE YOUNG

Seeing Steve at my Super Bowl party made me reflect on all the challenges he had faced. In 1984, I received a call from LeGrande Young, the father of BYU quarterback Steve Young, regarding representation. I knew they were lineal descendants of Brigham Young himself. I flew back to Greenwich, Connecticut, and met with the corporate attorney and his wife, Sherry. Ironically, I stayed in Steve's old room. The parents were bright and warm, and they had instilled strong values in their son. I felt an instant connection. I was scheduled to meet with Steve at the Salt Lake City airport.

People have always told me that I look much younger than my chronological age, and I certainly dress casually. I didn't see anyone who looked like a quarterback, though, and evidently Steve didn't see anyone who fit the agent stereotype. Eventually, I had him paged. We had been standing near each other the whole time.

Steve might well be the brightest athlete I have ever represented. He has a genius IQ—handsome, charismatic, and gifted, with a huge heart for helping people down on their luck. Steve was slated to be the first pick in the NFL draft as a franchise quarterback. He was a gifted athlete who played quarterback at BYU. He was the top-rated player overall among the 1984 NFL draft class. He was the beneficiary of a signing war between the NFL and the USFL, a fledgling league. Entering the USFL was merely a temporary move; he had dreamt of playing professional football in the NFL ever since he was a kid with a poster of Dallas quarterback Roger Staubach hanging over his bed. Steve believed in himself to actualize his dreams.

The Cincinnati Bengals would have selected him number one in the NFL draft, but they had an established starting quarterback in Ken Anderson. Instead, the Los Angeles Express of the USFL offered Steve the opportunity to begin immediately with a talented supporting cast and a coach with experience tutoring young quarterbacks. He signed a four-year, $42 million contract, the largest in the history of professional sports at the time. But his real motivation was not economic: Steve just wanted to play.

Steve understood the importance of patience, waiting for the right time to strike rather than act recklessly. It was the smarter decision to forgo the NFL and sign with the USFL temporarily, but neither of us was prepared for the difficult road ahead. The rug was pulled out from under our feet a year or so later when the USFL dissolved, leaving players high and dry. Because of the collapse, the NFL decided to hold a special supplemental draft for USFL players who were NFL-caliber. Steve was drafted number one overall by the Tampa Bay Buccaneers in 1985 and signed a multi-year contract. But there was a major stumbling block: the Buccaneers were the worst team in the NFL.

As a starter, he had little to no support from his team or fans. His biggest highlight was being sacked and driven into the snow in a game against the Green Bay Packers during a blizzard, when the Bucs were out of their depth, and Steve was sacked four times with zero TDs. Steve left the game, deemed the "Snow Bowl," with a picture of himself with a layer of ice over his face mask. It was truly a sight to be seen.

Despite their terrible record, we were excited to sign with the Bucs because they promised they'd take care of Steve on and off the field. While signing him as a quarterback, owner Hugh Culverhouse also planned to help Steve attend law school at Stetson University in the off-season. Steve's secondary career plans centered around law. He could handle a few rocky years because he saw the bigger picture.

The Bucs' horrendous year landed them the first pick in the draft, and they quickly grabbed the Heisman Trophy-winning quarterback Vinny Testaverde, a move that signaled the franchise had lost faith in Steve. Vinny was a talented quarterback at the

University of Miami and had fans across Florida. Talk about a shock. By drafting a local favorite, they had committed to Testaverde being their quarterback of the future. Had the Bucs forgotten all the promises they so recently made to us? They said that they wanted to build the team around Steve. Seeing the writing on the wall, we began brainstorming where we could get him traded next.

Culverhouse pledged to Steve and me that he would make up for broken promises by allowing Steve to decide which team he would play for next. Steve Young's primary concern was having an impact. He didn't want to spend time on the bench; he wanted to participate and have his time on the field. There were many teams interested in trading for him, but he was focused on the San Francisco 49ers. Steve had a private workout session with Bill Walsh, the 49ers' coach. Walsh was a guru at the quarterback position and had created a novel offensive scheme called the West Coast Offense. Bill told us that Joe Montana, the iconic Super Bowl-winning quarterback for his team, was retiring due to back problems.

Now, Joe Montana was the number-one quarterback in the league—a beloved icon in the Bay Area and a legend nationwide. Suddenly, Steve's path seemed to be back on track. He would be the perfect player to step into Joe's shoes.

He would only be replacing Montana because of Joe's back problem and need for retirement, so there would be no quarterback controversy. It was on this promise and this promise alone that Steve agreed to sign with the 49ers. On paper, starting with the 49ers seemed like a golden opportunity for Steve. They were a quarterback-centric team, led by the brilliant Bill Walsh and his innovative West Coast Offense, not to mention a multitude of great players. It should have been a slam dunk. The ideal situation. Except for the fact that Joe wasn't planning on retiring as we'd been told.

In fact, Bill Walsh's promise was greatly overstated because Joe took the news of Steve joining his team as a healthy dose of motivation. Suddenly, his back pain disappeared, and the veteran player swore he was in the best shape of his career. I would never have pushed for Steve to sign where he'd have to live in the shadows of an icon, if I'd known. At this point, Steve, one of the ten best quarterbacks in the league, was behind the best quarterback in all of football. What could he do now? His worst fears were actualized: he made it to the big leagues, but now he was blocked and frustrated.

He had to live through a series of seasons in which he watched from the bench, including two in which Montana led the 49ers to the Super Bowl. It was clear that Montana wasn't in love with the fact that a younger competitor was on his turf. Football is a competitive sport, and being the top QB on a team is what all quarterbacks strive for. Montana was a busy man with many demands. Having time to mentor and groom his successor wasn't at the top of his list. One day, Steve and I were out to dinner at a Chinese restaurant in Palo Alto, and he said to me, "I know I've been a disappointment to you because I'm a backup. You don't have to keep me as a client."

I told him he wasn't a disappointment, that I cherished our relationship, and that I would never think of ending it. My clients were like my kids. One may be more successful than another, but you love and support them all. Truth of the matter, I was glad he was transparent with me about how he was feeling. Though there wasn't much we could do at the time, we did begin conversations about it. But when Steve finally got into the game, he was immediately compared to Montana. And not the real Montana, but the fabricated ideal client, a product of euphoric recall that lived in the minds of the 49ers faithful of San Francisco. To them, Montana never threw an incomplete pass. Montana never threw an interception. Joe Montana was the perfect player, executing every play masterfully. If Montana did slip or fumble, the blame didn't fall on his shoulders; it fell on his team, the referees, or the opposing team. And Steve, on the other hand, was to be criticized for every mistake.

How did this gifted young athlete survive several years of sitting on the bench? How did he find the patience not to go stir crazy? He had strong support from a vast array of family and friends. He did not show his frustration publicly; he was always classy, but it was killing him inside. Instead of wasting time and brooding, Steve found a productive way to advance his life. He returned to BYU to earn his law degree during the off-season.

It was eventually clear that Steve was the future of the 49ers. After four years in the backup role, Steve finally got his chance when Montana suffered an elbow injury during the 1991 preseason. However, I feared he would never be judged on his own merits in the Bay Area but would always be compared unfavorably to the memory of Montana. And because of that, I suggested we look into trading him again. I thought the best plan of action was for him to go to another franchise where he'd be a starter and could finally start carving out his own destiny. Surprisingly, Steve was emphatic that he should stay with the 49ers. He was determined to be their starting quarterback. Steve thought there was something so unique about Bill Walsh and the West Coast Offense that, if he could just hold on long enough, he could have a series of great years. He could visualize his brighter tomorrow. He had faith in the coach, the system, and the supporting cast, which allowed him to sit for almost four years, attend law school, and remain patient.

As the starter, Steve showed the team and the NFL that he was always a star in the making as he blossomed into a quarterback. When Montana came back from his injury, the lingering question was who would stay and who would go. Montana was aging, but had led them to four Super Bowl wins with no losses. If there were a Mount Rushmore for NFL quarterbacks, his giant head would be chiseled in granite. No matter what the profession, cutting or trading a legend is never easy. But San Francisco could see the future in Steve Young, who was younger and ready to go. It was controversial in the Bay Area.

The big question ... would they ever trade Montana? I understood, it's hard to trade away someone who brought you so much. The uncertain potential that the next person would bring you something equal, or maybe even better, was a difficult situation to be in. In 1993, San Francisco made its decision: Montana was traded to the Kansas City Chiefs, but despite his absence, there was still deep allegiance to him in San Francisco as Steve finally joined the ranks as an NFL starting quarterback. It was an interesting time in San Francisco back then. Some people wanted to see Steve fail rather than for the 49ers to win. In the eyes of some fans, Steve held the sole responsibility for pushing Joe Montana out and into the Chiefs' awaiting arms.

In those first couple of years as a starter, Steve was constantly compared to Montana. It was like a ringing in our ears—the constant negativity aimed at him.

"Joe Montana would've never made that play!"

"Joe Montana would've never made that kind of pass!"

"Joe Montana would've never lost that game!"

The nagging and comparisons seemed never-ending! Eventually, the 49ers reached the Super Bowl in 1994 against the San Diego Chargers. This was Steve's golden moment on center stage. He dominated the Chargers, throwing six touchdown passes and earning MVP honors. I ran down on the field after the game, and he ran up and hugged me, shouting, "The monkey is off my back! The monkey is off my back!" Steve's ability to endure setbacks and remain committed to his dream led to his induction into the Football Hall of Fame in Canton, Ohio, in 2006.

Chapter 4

Courage: We Suffer, but We Survive

The monkey on my back was the constant string of misfortune in my private life. But the difference between Steve and me was that, during the lows, I found alcohol while he found education. He found a positive outlet to help him stay on track and keep him focused. I operated under the false belief that I could handle the lows on my own. While he was being transparent with me, I was totally hiding what I was going through.

I assumed that if I worked harder, put in more effort, and was more creative, I could protect my family and friends and continue to hide my struggle. But in retrospect, this belief was not inner strength; it was grandiosity. I thought that through my work, I could place indestructible, protective barriers around the people I loved. But this false sense of protection eroded when my dad received his cancer diagnosis. I remember the day he told me he had esophageal cancer like it was yesterday. On that day, the walls around me began to crumble slowly.

Suddenly, it was like I had my hands tied. Though I had huge financial resources, all the money in the world couldn't cure cancer. I wanted so badly to save my hero, but I couldn't. My father, the great Warren Steinberg, was larger than life. He was my role model. His tall stature, barrel chest, deep voice, and talented athleticism exuded strength, wisdom, and comfort. He redefined what it meant to be eighty. If he wasn't on the court playing tennis or out playing a round of golf, then he was spending time with his grandkids. In his elderly years, he was cognitively sharp, physically fit, and still someone I sought after for advice. Even today, I talk to him in my mind, wondering what he might do in certain situations I'm facing.

In short, he was one of the most courageous people I've ever known. When he was diagnosed, I thought the combination of my protective barrier and his great qualities would be enough to pull him through. But in reality, he began declining during the harsh treatment of chemotherapy, each time getting weaker and weaker. Suddenly, the man who was always bigger than me started losing weight. He tried to act like his usual self, still dispensing wisdom in common-sense terms. He was the person I went to when I had doubts and fears. I'd tell him, "Dad, I'm starting to pick up weight, what do I do?" He'd just smile and suggest, "Why don't you get some bigger pants?"

When I was a fresh law school graduate, I remember worrying about failing my California Bar Exam.

"Are you studying for it?" he'd ask. "Yes," I answered.

"Did you pay the fee for it?" "Yes," I answered.

"What's the worst thing that can happen?" "Well, I could fail."

"You won't know till you take it."

That was how he tackled the challenges of life, great and small: with bravery. I was less brave. His suffering was reflected in his skin and his eyes. I did my best to be strong and positive at all times. I really believed he would beat cancer and outlive us all, but inside, I was totally destabilized. I held my composure at the time, but deep down, I think my father knew by the way he would look at me. My father died in 2004 after entering remission for a brief period. The month before his death, he attended my eldest son's high school graduation. He also received an award from the Human Relations Commission of Los Angeles for Outstanding Leadership in Fighting Racism. Even sick, he still served as my North Star.

At the funeral, I said, "He taught us how to live, and he taught us how to die." His death crushed me. But it was the vodka that blotted out the pain. I listened and drank some more to wash away the pain I felt. Like many people who are suffering from anything ranging from depression to alcohol abuse, I was afraid to open up to people about the turmoil that was living inside of me. When my father passed away, I never expended focus on expiating the grief it had brought.

I self-medicated with more vodka. I bottled up my emotions rather than deal with the hurt. I took on way too much responsibility. I arranged my father's funeral and ensured everyone else's needs were met. I comforted my mother and my children and resisted comfort from others. My father's death weighed heavily on my shoulders. My body needed self-reflection and the chance to maneuver through the hurt and grief. But I let the duties of being the eldest son fool me into believing I could support the world's weight. I was slowly crumbling inside, but felt like everyone expected me to be strong, so I did my best to bury my true emotions.

Shortly after the funeral, my eldest son, Jon, was diagnosed with retinitis pigmentosa, a rare and incurable eye disease that causes blindness. It was a slow and gradual descent, beginning as nighttime blindness that narrows visual fields, ultimately resulting in total blindness. Before the diagnosis, Jon was on the fast track to a career as a sports broadcaster. He enjoyed being a radio host, gifted writer, and novelist during college.

While I fretted and drank, Jon reacted to his diagnosis with optimism, focusing on what he still could do, creating and executing a bucket list, and eventually working in a center for training younger blind individuals. This should have shown me the right way to react. He went back to Saint Mary's College and earned two master's degrees in creative writing. That, too, was courageous. But I didn't emulate that courage. The pain of my son's diagnosis cut deep for me. I felt like the biblical figure Job, who faced multiple challenges that brought suffering, or like the

Egyptians who suffered plague after plague as Moses fought to free his people from slavery. I wondered what would be next: boils, locusts, or flies. The pain and pressure felt like boom, boom, boom all over my body.

Even in the face of uncertainty, I wanted my son to live on the side of optimism. The glass is half full, not half empty. But internally, I was completely and utterly distraught. This wasn't something I could outwit or outwork. I had to sit and watch as this invisible enemy destroyed his vision. My son was the one with the diagnosis, but he maintained a positive outlook throughout. I, on the other hand, completely personalized his diagnosis.

In 2001, my family had the house of our dreams. Planted on a double lot, it was equipped with the perfect playhouse for my daughter, a fort for my sons, an Olympic-size pool, and a breathtaking view of the Pacific Ocean in Newport Beach. It was picture-perfect until a torrential downpour flooded our home. After the storm passed, we thought we had cleaned up most of the water and remediated the flooring, but then my wife and son suddenly suffered from a respiratory infection. At my brother's wedding in Virginia, we met one of his friends, who had experienced one of the first outbreaks of mold in Austin, Texas. She strongly recommended that we have our house tested for mold. To our shock, the test revealed high levels of stachybotrys mold, also known as black or toxic mold, and other dangerous molds that had circulated throughout our house via the air conditioner. We were advised that we had to leave within twenty-four hours due to the severity of the health risks. We left all of our belongings in the house, fearing that they were contaminated. We left with the clothes on our backs and headed directly to temporary housing. We then began our tedious search for a new home.

While we were living in temporary housing, we did not want the responsibility of selling a house with mold to a new buyer, so we knocked the house to the ground and sold it as a lot. We then found a new home in Newport Beach that was ostensibly mold-proof. This perfect house gave us a wonderful lifestyle for a couple of years, but then another torrential rainstorm hit, and it turned out that our house and the adjacent houses had a roof defect. Remarkably, we had the same mold problem all over again. My job as a father was to provide safe housing for my family, yet the complete opposite was happening.

This put even more strain on my family and, even more so, on my marriage. By the fall of 2006, the stress of losing our home leaked into my marriage and, before I knew it, I was signing divorce papers with my ex-wife. From the house to the divorce was like living in a whirlwind pyramid. For my part, I wish I had communicated more effectively with my wife.

With each misstep, I was setting myself farther off course and deeper into the hands of alcoholism. My string of misfortunes did not begin my battle against the bottle, but it acted as its fuel. The hurt and pain steered me from my foundational roots and sent me on a crash course.

It was ironic: I had spent years counseling athletes and friends, helping them navigate their own challenges, offering insight, solutions, and strength. Yet I lacked the self-awareness to recognize how desperately I needed help. I wasn't ready to face the truth, let alone admit it out loud. I wasn't ready to demonstrate the vulnerability of acknowledging I'd lost control. Every journey is filled with peaks and valleys, but how could I help others find healing when I was running on empty? How could I focus on anyone else's wellbeing when I was quietly unraveling?

Substances don't work. I had tried that route. They only numb the pain temporarily, pushing the truth further into the background. What I really needed was strength: the kind that lives deep inside you. The kind that holds firm when the world feels like it's falling apart. The kind that says, "No matter how much agony I'm in, I won't back down."

But here's the truth most people don't talk about: strength isn't always loud. It doesn't always look like standing tall or charging forward. Sometimes, strength is soft. Sometimes, it's admitting you're scared. It's having the courage to say, "I don't have this all figured out." It's asking for help. That was the turning point, when I began to understand a different kind of courage. One that doesn't come from pretending to have it all together, but from being willing to be vulnerable and let others in.

VULNERABILITY

Vulnerability is that kind of courage. And it became one of the most important values I learned on my comeback journey. Some think being vulnerable means being weak. On the contrary, it is a sign of strength. It takes a lot of courage to open yourself up to others, share your feelings, acknowledge your fears, and ask for help. Today, we are so closed off from one another. Digital technology and social media amplify this alienation; in a counterintuitive way, we're all intimately and globally connected, and yet so distant and reclusive. Many of us live in a bubble, letting others and outside forces tell us how to think and act. Instead of acting with courage, we become fearful of the outside world, the world beyond the screen. Many people instead find a way to divide rather than come together.

Social media runs the world. Do not make the mistake of comparing yourself to the rest of the world's presentation online. It is not a clear representation of the challenges we humans face in life: depression, marital problems, and economic hardship. Comparing yourself to others and making yourself feel as if you are less than is not helpful on either the road to a comeback or in everyday life.

Connectivity builds foundational relationships. When we are at our lowest points in life, it is crucial to avoid bottling up our emotions. Vulnerability is one of life's hardest skills, yet it brings such beauty. When we are vulnerable, people are eager to meet us with grace and compassion. There are moments we need to be open with those who care for us. I think it is only human to be tempted to cover up mistakes through misrepresentation out of fear of public perception or judgment. Many times, we feel pressured to be perfect, to put on a brave face; we are afraid to unmask ourselves out of fear of others' scrutiny. We all have to realize that the world is not perfect, and nor are we. I saw things differently once I was able to be transparent about my mental health.

Many of the great stories in religious faiths are about people being transparent and overcoming injustice to help humanity. No matter what the struggle is in life, you will need someone to help pull you up that mountain. Don't try to be a one-person show. This life was not made to be lived alone.

I get that it's hard to spill your heart out to a friend. Typically, we all like to guard ourselves from judgment. And that judgment is why transparency can seem so threatening. The fear of not living up to others' expectations is a major reason people avoid transparency. Whether you're a public figure or not, people have set beliefs about who you are, and we sometimes feel the need to align with these standards.

It's never easy to admit when we're struggling. You have to just remember that accepting your struggle is not a bad thing; it is the first step to getting your life in order on your comeback journey. Men appear to have a more difficult time revealing their deep emotions than women do. Men are taught to be stoic. Vulnerability is taboo. Most men often shy away from conversations in which they might bare their souls or reveal their doubts. From childhood to adulthood, little boys are given less space to explore and share their feelings because they may be picked on for being sensitive. These boys then grow up never learning the skill of discussing and processing their emotions.

The average man could have just found out that his wife is leaving him or that he was diagnosed with stage four cancer, and if you were to walk up to him in the middle of the street and ask him about his day, he'd reply, "Everything's fine!" While two men talking presents the opportunity for shared problems, the more men present in any situation, the less likely it is that anyone will ever cut below the surface. As a man, a father, and a leader, I understand the pressure to always come across as having everything under control. But that kind of mentality is what kept me in denial and from swallowing my truth. Many people see wealthy, famous people and assume their lives are perfect. Making it to the top of any profession is a huge undertaking and, along the way, there are a lot of bumps in the road that challenge you mentally. Take, for example, Dwayne "The Rock" Johnson, a physical marvel with seemingly endless self-confidence, who has built an illustrious career playing loveable tough guys and has become a major box-office star.

For years, The Rock struggled with depression. Having gone through family hardships, followed by his pro football dreams shattering due to injuries, and failing in school, he fell down a dark road of depression. The Rock feared never finding a way back to normalcy and worried that, if things didn't change, he might become suicidal like his mother. Like most people, at first his pride prevented him from sharing his feelings. He was the golden child who was supposed to make it and support his family. When life's struggles stepped in the way, he was devastated.

"Struggle and pain are real. I was devastated and depressed," The Rock said in a 2018 interview with The Daily Express. "I reached a point where I didn't want to do a thing or go anywhere. I was crying constantly. Took me a long time to realize it, but the key is not to be afraid to open up." If it wasn't for him being transparent and accepting of his condition, The Rock might not have ever found his way back. And we, as fans, might have never met him or witnessed his talents. The Rock is an example of transparency as an act of courage in and of itself.

KERRI STRUG AND SIMONE BILES

Having represented numerous athletes, one in particular reminds me that the tiniest people are often the most dauntless. Bold acts of bravery come in small packages. Every pro athlete has a moment, usually many, when they must courageously push through the pain. Few have done that as memorably or inspiringly as my gymnast client Kerri Strug. Eighteen-year-old Kerri qualified for the 1996 Olympics. Though the USA had home advantage as the Olympics were in Atlanta that year, the cards seemed stacked against the United States team. Russian gymnasts had dominated the sport for years prior and were the sure favorite. But our team was dubbed the Magnificent Seven and determined to strive for the gold.

In the finals, the women's team was leading by less than a point against the competition, and it was all coming down to the final event—the vault. Four of Kerri's teammates went before her and left the mat with disappointing performances. To only make matters worse, fourteen-year-old Dominique Moceanu stepped up to the vault and managed to fall on both of her turns.

I can only imagine the overbearing amount of pressure Kerri must have felt at that moment. Here they were, inches away from taking the gold home for the very first time as a team, but they needed the points from Kerri's next vault. The gold medal stood not only for Kerri but for the entire United States. As Kerri stepped up to the vault, she took a deep breath and, feeling the eyes of the world watching her, began her routine. But then Kerri tumbled to the floor, spraining her ankle in the process. The world watched as she pulled herself together and limped her way back, wincing.

She looked at her coach and said, "Do we need this to win?" The answer was yes.

Kerri approached the vault again. With enormous grace and courage, she tossed her body into the air and landed perfectly, hitting the ground simultaneously with both feet. Her face was twisted in agony. She'd done it—America had won the gold medal.

There is an iconic picture of Kerri being carried off the mat by her coach, Bela Karolyi, with a leg cast on, her gold medal swinging around her neck. She went on to become an American hero that summer, appearing with legendary comedian Bob Hope on the "Family Film Awards," touring around the country and conducting interviews. She was praised for her bravery and resiliency.

What happened next after this bold, fearless act? The challenge in representing an Olympic athlete is that they have a dramatic moment on the worldwide stage and then their sport does not have much exposure again until the next Olympics. So, we had to be creative in extending Kerri's shelf life. She appeared on Barbara Walters' special of "The Most Interesting People," handed out an award with Bob Hope, rang the bell to open up Wall Street trading, and was carried out onto the field by AOL president Steve Case at halftime on Monday Night Football.

The TV show Saturday Night Live featured a skit by comedian Chris Kattan, which satirized her high voice. We helped Kerri create her own gymnastics show, which toured the country. She also made a deal with Disney on Ice to hold exhibitions on the side of the rink. She then retired and returned to UCLA and Stanford, where she earned a master's degree in psychology. She's been very productive working in the general counsel's office in the Treasury Department and the Justice Department of Juvenile Justice. She's also competed in a series of marathons. Kerri's life clearly did not end on the floor. It was only getting started.

All this was due to a grand act of courage on the world stage, under enormous pressure. But I know Kerri didn't do it for personal gain. She did it for her team. She did it because that's what athletes do: rise to the challenge. In 2021, Simone Biles faced a different situation. During the Olympics, Simone developed something called the "twisties," meaning she had lost the ability to control her jumps. In the air, she could no longer gauge where her body was in relation to the mat, so she made the difficult decision to withdraw from the Olympics. The backlash was immediate.

She was branded as a quitter, belittled, and bullied by those who once supported her, just for putting her mental health and well-being first. Simone stood her ground and refused to be intimidated by people advising her to push on. In some respects, she made the opposite choice to Kerri Strug. If Kerri was brave, does that mean Simone was a coward? If you listened to the relentless chorus of online and press critics, you might have said yes.

But one voice stood above the rest of the negativity: Kerri publicly defended Simone and her decision. She understood just how important it was for Simone to be transparent with herself and not give in to the pressure of hiding her true feelings from others. Simone's act took courage, too. Most people would not have the fortitude to bow out at that moment. The Olympics are a historic event that only happens every four years, and getting back is never a guarantee. But Simone chose her health over winning a gold medal. She listened to herself, not to the noise of others, and presented her truth. I applauded Simone for her bravery and Kerri for her support. It's okay to lose the battle if that means winning the war. Simone Biles understood this concept when she said, "There's life after gymnastics."

She wasn't willing to risk a lifelong injury; she could see the bigger picture. Simone's resilience led to a very happy ending. She came back and made the US women's gymnastics team for the 2024 Paris Olympics. She won three gold medals and one silver medal, earning the title of overall best gymnast, and inspired a whole generation of young girls to match her resolve. Simone showed everyone why she is considered the world's greatest gymnast.

In times of stress, do not feel like you must be the sole column that holds up the building. It's okay to admit to the addiction or the issue that is troubling you; it's okay to reach out for help. You don't always have to display strength. In fact, the real strength is being honest about where you're at in life and reaching out when in need of assistance.

Chapter 5

Hope: It Ain't Over till It's Over

During my struggles, I always envisioned returning to my authentic self. I so desperately wanted to get my heart back to where it once was, because I quickly learned that nothing can get you moving forward if your heart isn't in it. All of my, what I like to call, false starts to my recovery were due to that: I just wasn't ready. My mind thought I was, but my heart was not. Sometimes it takes time for our mind and heart to align.

Whether it's a comeback or something in everyday life, like doing well at work, make sure your heart is in it and that you are doing it for the right reasons. Your purpose should not be for others, but for the greater good of improving yourself. This is similar to an airline attendant telling you to put on your own air mask before putting one on your child or another person. How can you help someone else if you are barely surviving? I think the quote from Uncle Ben in the Spider-Man movie was, "With great power comes great responsibility." In our world, most of us have great power, but many of us fail at taking responsibility. I had to see my existence as a matter of life and death. When people told me my drinking could kill me, I looked at them in bewilderment. I had too little fear of the consequences, and here my optimism worked against me. I needed to be shocked into breaking denial and facing reality.

While I appreciated the outside motivation, in the end, it was not enough. My inner drive to become sober had to be ignited in myself. I had to hit rock bottom to find my inner strength. Nobody knows your inner strength better than you. You have to be the leader on your comeback trail to recovery. Don't be deterred by barriers. Obstacles are inevitable. Setbacks are part of the game. Your inner strength, your hope, is what enables you to power through. No matter how big the obstacle, know that you can overcome it.

You have to believe in yourself, and believing in yourself means believing the future will be brighter. When addicts reach rock bottom, it is often accompanied by a feeling of despair—how will I ever get out of this? When you're deep in the pit, it is hard to imagine finding a way to climb back out. But maintaining hope is indispensable.

That's the little spark that ignites the engine inside you. And sometimes, when you've lost everything, hope might be all you have.

JUNE JONES

No one had a better understanding of what it means to be optimistic in the face of adversity than my dear friend and client, Coach June Jones. I met June Jones when he was a quarterback backing up starter Steve Bartkowski in 1976. June was brilliant with a vision for the future. Little did I know back then that one day he'd be a saving grace for me.

June played college football at Oregon, Hawaii, and Portland State, where he distinguished himself as a savant when it came to understanding the quarterback position. At Portland State, he and head coach Mouse Davis developed a new offense called the run-and-shoot. Today, the run-and-shoot, although known by many names, is used in some form by virtually every NFL team. But back then, it was visionary.

The run-and-shoot has changed the way football is played as we know it today. In this offense, rather than having two running backs, you scale back to one. There are multiple eligible receivers, and the key is to focus on passing. June helped shape the modern-day football game that you and I are accustomed to by championing the run-and-shoot offense throughout his coaching career.

He was a faith-based Christian man with great intelligence and creativity. Because he was a scratch golfer, he was constantly forming relationships with businessmen in a variety of new enterprises. I took June on as a client and helped him through his transition from the field to coaching. He started as the receivers coach for the Houston Gamblers, then landed his first NFL gig as the quarterback coach for the Atlanta Falcons. He then became the head coach of the Falcons and the interim head coach of the San Diego Chargers.

It was no surprise when the San Diego Chargers offered him a seven-figure, multi-year contract to stay with the team. Normally, we'd sign in an instant, but June hesitated when he found out that Hawaii had an opening for the head coach spot. He fell in love with everything about Hawaii when he played there in college, and he had fond memories of surfing every morning.

"Well, what do I do?" June asked me for advice one day. "I can't decide between the Chargers and Hawaii. The Chargers are a better deal, but Hawaii has my heart."

Conventional NFL wisdom holds that being a head coach is the highest attainable position in the game. He didn't realize it at the time, but June didn't need my guidance; he'd already answered his own question. His heart was with Hawaii. Hawaii was home.

"Many people will judge you for not accepting the Chargers' offer, but that's not important. You only have this one lifetime, and what matters is that you follow your heart," I told him.

Now, this is not a picture of hopefulness amidst despair. Things were going well for June. His optimism was evident in his belief that he could thrive in these circumstances, despite being far from the high-flying glitz and glamor of leading a storied NFL franchise. Hawaii offered only $400,000 in salary and had poor facilities and not enough money in its recruiting budget to bring players from the mainland. Bigger, flashier schools, such as the University of Oregon, were a more attractive draw for top players. Hawaii quarterback Colt Brennan complained that there wasn't enough soap in the locker room to take a shower. June would have to use his own video camera to tape plays because Hawaii didn't offer any game footage.

And this was reflected in the team's on-the-field performance. When he accepted the position, he was agreeing to run a squad that had posted an astonishing 0-11 record the previous year—a winless, talentless team with a "BYOS" (Bring Your Own Soap) policy. June had an uphill battle to face.

As the new coach, he had to figure out how to turn the program around. How easy would it have been for June to become overwhelmed by this herculean task and throw in the towel? He could have given up and landed a lavish role in the NFL. But instead, he stepped up his game. In June's first year, employing a heavy brew of island juju and his Christian faith, he motivated his roster to peak performance. Hawaii went from 0-11 to 9-4, which was one of the fastest turnarounds in college football history. That lesson would stay with June when he faced the biggest challenge of his life, one greater and more high-stakes than resurrecting an underperforming college team.

One night, June fell asleep at the wheel on the freeway. His car collided with a concrete stanchion; the impact pummeled his body, shattering sixteen bones and causing a separated aorta. Most people would have bled out and died right there, but June woke up in the hospital, in agony, but alive.

It was fortunate that years of playing football had conditioned his body. Only athletes with the rare ability to endure and absorb extreme levels of pain can withstand the relentless toll of football. Their rehabilitation capacity is far higher than that of the average human being. One day, I visited quarterback Troy Aikman at the hospital after he had back disk surgery. Remarkably, he was up and walking around.

I asked, "Did the doctor say you should be up?" He responded, "No, but isn't it great?"

Troy's ability to bounce back quickly reminded me of June.

June's prognosis was dire. The doctors said it would take him six years to fully recover. Now, on top of rebuilding a team, he had to rebuild his body.

Despite his grim predicament, not only did June heal, but he somehow found the strength to return to the sidelines in less than six months. Remarkably, he led the Warriors to be the only undefeated regular-season team in Division 1 that year, which also turned out to be his last year of coaching at Hawaii. What a turnaround from 0-11. In June's case, his faith in God was his guiding light. He believed that Jesus was looking out for him. Even though he was sitting in bed with his body shattered, he believed that he could come back.

One of the steps in the recovery program that I follow says, "Make the decision to turn your will and life over to the care of God as you understand him." In the face of adversity, when the path forward seems too daunting to overcome, you have to dig deep and find an internal belief in yourself and in a higher power.

A belief so strong that, despite the current situation, you are confident that you will make it to a better tomorrow. June Jones had to have that same faith. That intervention by a higher power and his belief in God would lead him to better circumstances.

Many people draw hope from their faith. But you don't have to be Christian or even adhere to any organized religion. It may be a belief in another higher power or spiritual force. Although some people struggle with accepting God, the point is that you can't handle the problem alone. This life was not made to be lived alone. It's a hard truth to swallow, but your single-minded thinking might be how you landed in this situation in the first place. You have to rely not on your own brain but instead on your relationship with a higher power. I believe there's a spirit in the world that can't be measured rationally. This spirit connects and operates to help us trust the goodness of people and the ability to change.

It's that same spirit that gives Iranian women the strength to stand up against a repressive theocratic regime in the hopes of a better tomorrow. This is where reliance on a higher power's strength and guidance is critical. It's the same spirit that gives a mother in a tough neighborhood the willpower to toil at two jobs to provide for her children. Maintaining hope that, by the strength of your will and the grace of God (however you imagine God to be), you will break out of the darkness and into the light. There's a spirit inside of us that can move mountains. If you're an addict, it is tempting to numb the pain and look for fleeting, chemically induced "hope" in a bottle or a pill. But that will only compound your problems. Hope comes from within (your strength of spirit) and without (the faith you derive from the support of family, friends, and/or a higher power), but it can't be manufactured with a substance.

Fear is a natural part of the process of coming back. It is part of the human condition. But unchecked fear can eat away at hope. There is a scene in Rocky III, when Apollo Creed is training Rocky on the beach to fight Clubber Lane in a rematch, after Clubber had knocked Rocky out. Rocky wasn't motivated and was just going through the motions. Frustrated, Apollo demanded Rocky tell him what was wrong before he walked off. Then Rocky's wife went to him and asked him what was going on. Hesitantly, Rocky finally replied, "I'm afraid."

Fear is the number one driver for success and failure. It hinders us from taking those risks necessary for success. We become afraid of the unknown and would rather never try than face the issue head-on. Do not let the fear of striking out keep you from being the person you want to be. One of my dad's great heroes was President Franklin D. Roosevelt, who said, "We have always held to the hope, the belief, the conviction that there is a better life, a better world, beyond the horizon." One of my dad's secret tools was his overwhelmingly optimistic outlook on life. He could find hope in the worst situations. Even when something bad happened to my father when we were growing up, or even when he got cancer, he never let you feel sorry for him. He was always more concerned about the people around him than himself. His spirit was so pure; his service to the community and the world was from his heart.

There is another source of hope which you can always tap into, what I like to call "proportionality." This is the notion that, no matter how bad you have it, things could be a lot worse. It's the act of taking stock of your situation and, rather than dwelling on everything that is going wrong, counting your blessings.

Sure, when you're in the doldrums and nothing is going right, it might sound like a fool's errand. Maybe you only have one or two blessings to count. But many of us overreact to our own problems, such that we blow them all out of proportion in our heads. When I was struggling, I experienced a revelation one day in the park. Yes, I had fallen from grace, reduced to drinking paper bag vodka on a bench a block from my childhood home. But as I looked around, certain truths struck me: my life was in turmoil, but at least I could sit here in peace, in a free and democratic country. I was not a starving peasant in a third-world country. My last name wasn't Steinberg in Nazi Germany in the thirties. My health had been affected, but I didn't have cancer or an incurable illness. I was able to stay active. I still had family who loved me, even if those relationships had suffered.

In this light, my problems, grave as they were, were suddenly diminished, like when the monster of your childhood nightmares shrinks as soon as you muster the courage to stare it right in the eye. I had a lot to be thankful for. And I had the basic conditions to make a change, if I could find the strength to do so, without giving in to despair. That was a game-changer. Proportionality, keeping things in perspective, is so important when you are faced with a potentially life-ruining or life-ending crisis. One story that comes to mind is the battle that Robin Roberts had with breast cancer and myelodysplastic syndrome (MDS), a rare blood and bone marrow disorder.

Back in 2007, Robin was diagnosed with triple-negative breast cancer. Instead of hiding in a corner, Robin announced her diagnosis to the world. She faced it head-on and gave the world a front-row seat. She courageously went through surgery, chemotherapy, and radiation treatments. She even had her head shaved on Good Morning America while her fans watched. But one of the most valuable things we saw during that time was not just a woman fighting for her life, but a person willing to be open about something they could have easily kept quiet.

She made her comeback a learning experience for people. GMA had segments on mammograms, ultrasounds, and MRIs as tools for early detection of the disease. I'm sure those informational segments helped millions of women not only understand the disease and provide preventive methods but also support one another.

Then five years later, after beating breast cancer, she got diagnosed with myelodysplastic syndrome. I can imagine her screaming at the ceiling, asking, "Why me?" But Robin, once again, faced her diagnosis with courage. Thankfully, she had a sister who was a perfect match, and she underwent a successful bone marrow transplant operation that saved her life, yet again. Robin faced the reality of her situation and refused to yield to pessimism, even when it was the path of least resistance. It's easier to be grim and brooding about your prospects, but it takes strength to be a stalwart optimist in the face of hardship. Which, I suppose, is why most people aren't, but Robin's optimism helped her survive.

Note that hope does not mean denying the reality of your situation. On the contrary, being uncomfortable with our pain and refusing to grapple with it on a spiritual or psychological level is the barrier that prevents us from seeing the truth. Rather than running away from the hurt, lean into it. Embrace it and watch as the fear and pain dissipate around you. Are you moving through life trying to forget the loved one you lost? When a memory arises, do you scramble to quickly find the nearest distraction? It's okay, I've been there.

It's a phrase we repeat but still seem to forget. We as humans are emotional beings, meaning we have the capacity to range from pure euphoric joy and happiness, while also reaching immobilizing and gut-punching sadness. We must learn to coexist with both. Hope and willingness are inextricably intertwined. Anything you are trying to accomplish in this world starts with the hope that you will overcome a challenge and succeed. Hope is a pillar of life on earth, and it's the reason people get up each day, hoping today will be better than the day before. For my recovery, I spent countless hours hoping at night that in the morning I would be the man I was raised to be. To snap my fingers and magically cure this affliction. But hope is only part of the bigger picture—you must have the willingness to focus and give your all into turning that hope into reality to beat whatever demon you are fighting. I found the hope that I could achieve sobriety, and I know you can see the hope you need in your life, too.

Chapter 6

Accountability: Step Up or Sit Out

There are many avenues to try to achieve sobriety. The first, and most well-known, option is checking into a rehabilitation facility. Patients are sent to a center to complete a thirty-, sixty-, or ninety-day program. The first part of the program is an intense detox, generally employing the use of Valium or other calming medicines. The treatment center monitors blood pressure and ensures patients don't undergo any medical issues that arise from weaning themselves off a substance their body is hooked on. Before my crash, I opted for this route, but these facilities come with a hefty price tag that I couldn't afford. Still, I couldn't do it alone. I needed the support of a facility with the resources and staff who are experts in helping people like me.

Following my epiphany on my father's bed, I called my brother Jim, who had been my steadfast supporter. I was ready to accept help. Jim traveled to our family's home, and he and my sponsor at the time, Bill Long, put their heads together to try to figure out the most effective treatment plan.

Given my financial constraints, a pristine, high-priced rehab center wasn't an option. So, we headed to a recovery center called Charle Street. Charle Street "First Step House of Orange County" is a short-term residential facility for indigent men. Instead of a stay of several weeks or months, it's a ten-day program that doesn't use medication to help ease the pain of detoxification. Instead, the program strives to provide a sober community to kickstart the journey back into the real world. It's rough, but it's effective. And I didn't really have any other options.

However, to my ignominious misfortune, Charle Street did not have a bed available, and I couldn't check in. Talk about a truly humbling experience. Even the home for the indigent was turning me away! Enduring humbling moments is par for the course on the road to recovery. You have to swallow your pride. Humility is a virtue in general, but a shield for the warriors fighting for a comeback.

During a visit to Charle Street, I met Kevin Y., who ran a sober living house. With his help, I landed a bed at his home in Orange, California. A sober living house refers to any place of residence that bridges the inpatient recovery experience with the "real world." It's essentially a halfway house that gives recovering addicts the opportunity to take the hard work they've done in inpatient recovery and apply it to real-life situations. It helps with your transition back to your regular life so that you can adjust to daily life and its challenges. They help you maintain healthy living habits and find activities that enable you to get on your feet. And they do what they can to keep you away from the bottle. But at sober living, that dangerous freedom doesn't exist, for our own good.

They hold you accountable, even on days when you just want to be left alone, don't want to see anyone, and don't want anyone telling you what to do. Some comebacks need allies to hold your hand and keep you on track when your own discipline falters.

Unlike other rehab centers, one can stay in a sober living house as long as they see fit. From four months to a couple of years, however long it takes to establish a baseline of sobriety. Usually, sober living houses have ten to fifteen beds where four men bunk together, but I had my own room because of my age. I know from the outside looking in that transitioning back to complete independence from your sober living community may seem easy. Still, the reality of it all is that, commonly, people recovering from addiction fall back into old habits.

According to therecoveryvillage.com, eighty percent of people who attempt to stop drinking relapse in their first year of sobriety. Overall, more than seventy percent of people suffering from alcoholism will relapse at some point in their recovery. That's why developing tools for success is critical as you build a new life around sobriety. Adapting to sober living was anything but easy. After checking in, I collapsed in my bed and fell into hibernation. When I woke up and started reading the Los Angeles Times, the paper was dated Sunday, even though I checked in on Friday.

I'd been asleep for the entire weekend. In the first couple of weeks without drinking, the body is so relieved by the lack of alcohol that you enter something called a "pink cloud." It's a brief period where you feel normal and even euphoric, but after some time, the cravings come back. That is why getting through the first month or two of sobriety is critical because later in the process, the cravings disappear. It turned out that, with a few exceptions, the sober living house did not provide regular meals, and I didn't have money for groceries. I was reduced to a state where I'd go back to Charle Street to grab candy bars. Some of the guys I met at meetings would take me to lunch now and then. Life at sober living exposed me to how easily people could become homeless. There's a thin line between stability and survival. A few bad breaks, no safety net, and lacking family support, you can find yourself sleeping under an overpass, wondering how you got there. That realization stayed with me.

It was a sobering wake up call, not just about how close I'd come to the edge. Sober living was my saving grace. Sober living encouraged us to find outside employment, and I was in desperate need of money, so job hunting I went. I put together a nice resume and decided that, since I had a love of books and all things literature, I'd apply to work at the local Barnes & Noble. At the first bookstore I tried, I slid my resume over to the manager.

"We can't hire you, Mr. Steinberg. We remember you from your book tour and do not want a celebrity operating the check-out stand!" he said, pushing my resume back into my hands.

And at the second Barnes & Noble, I was met with, "Are you kidding me? You're a lawyer? You're going to try and run the place!"

It was frustrating. I felt defeated after each rejection. I almost began to question how I was going to even get my head above water to afford food for myself. Just when I felt like I was making some progress, I asked myself if I had simply replaced one rut with another. Those initial days at sober living felt like an extension of rock bottom. It was hard to imagine a brighter day. But I had to remember that I was raised with endless optimism and could see the light at the end of the tunnel. I couldn't give up. It was time to start being accountable to myself and my own health and wellness.

Being accountable is one of the easiest concepts to profess, but the struggle of alcoholism makes it easy for alcoholics to blame others for their problems. Most people hate being wrong or admitting that they didn't complete a task. I view accountability as the glue that connects commitment to results. When you become more transparent about who you are or what you are trying to do, people will see you as more credible.

This time around, I exposed myself to the world. I wanted to kick the addiction and be the best person I could be. The person my parents raised me to be—a person who fights for the underprivileged and those with no voice. That person was still alive inside of me. So, if it meant staying in sober living and living off candy bars for some time, then that's what I was going to do.

The first imperative of recovery is breaking the pattern of denial and the disease that fools you into believing you do not have a disease. It was checking into sober living and beginning the same process I'd failed so many times before. If you're an alcoholic or suffering from some type of addiction, maybe you have your own list of rehab centers you've frequented. Perhaps you've hit rock bottom not because of an addiction but another affliction.

Regardless of the affliction, remember who you're accountable to, and include yourself on the list. No matter how hard it is, or how long the journey seems, don't you deserve to try again? To give it another attempt? You have a responsibility to yourself not to give up and to keep fighting. One way to start holding yourself accountable is to form a consistent pattern—something that repeats every single day and keeps you on track toward your goal. Consistency helps you stay in the moment rather than become frantic about the end goal. Remember that years of abuse or addiction cannot be conquered in a day, a week, or in most instances, a year. Fighting addiction is a lifetime struggle that requires you to keep your guard up, and it necessitates continuously refreshing your defenses.

For example, start your day with a motivating prayer or journal to help get your thoughts out on paper. Schedule a set time to exercise, like a daily jog or yoga class. Maybe you need to practice mindfulness and experiment with meditation. Meditation's effects on mood and well-being are well-documented. Meditation ultimately gives the brain a rest, helps achieve a state of peace, and helps individuals conquer more than they can imagine.

Comebacks are not achieved with sheer, raw motivation alone, because some days, you simply won't feel that motivation. Consistency and self-discipline are the mortar that holds the bricks together. You can't force yourself to be motivated, but you can basically will yourself to stick to a schedule or a pattern of behavior.

What event or pattern can you add to your life to stay consistent in your comeback? Even as I am about to hit sixteen years in my sobriety, I have changed virtually nothing. I have a morning routine. I still attend the same recovery meetings and do not miss meetings with my home group. I read the same literature, stay consistent with my sponsor, and continually work on the Twelve Steps. The most critical source document is The Big Book, which outlines the program and its steps. Here are the invaluable Twelve Steps for anyone suffering from alcohol addiction:

1. We admitted we were powerless over alcohol—that our lives had become unmanageable.

2. Came to believe that a Power greater than ourselves could restore us to sanity.

3. Decided to turn our will and our lives over to the care of God as we understood Him.

4. Made a searching and fearless moral inventory of ourselves.

5. Admitted to God, to ourselves, and to another human being the exact nature of our wrongs.

6. We are entirely ready to have God remove all these defects of character.

7. Humbly asked Him to remove our shortcomings.

8. Made a list of all persons we had harmed and became willing to make amends to them all.

9. Made direct amends to such people wherever possible, except when to do so would injure them or others.

10. Continued to take personal inventory and, when we were wrong, promptly admitted it.

11. Sought through prayer and meditation to improve our conscious contact with God as we understood Him, praying only for knowledge of His will for us and the power to carry that out.

12. Having had a spiritual awakening as a result of these steps, we tried to carry this message to alcoholics and to practice these principles in all our affairs.

I began to attend other recovery-oriented events and still do. There was an Orange County Men's Banquet, a desert weekend in Palm Springs, California, called the "Pow-Wow." Thousands of recovered alcoholics attended from all around the world. Another event I participated in that year was an International Convention in San Antonio. At the end, they asked attendees with long-term sobriety to rise as they tallied off the milestones: forty years, fifty years, sixty years. When attendees stood proudly to show they had been sober for six decades, the crowd went wild. What an inspiration for a newcomer. Although I felt it was presumptuous to be professing knowledge of recovery so early, people in the recovery community started asking me to speak at different meetings and events. Early in my sobriety, people asked me to sponsor them.

As I moved forward on my comeback trail and became more accountable to myself and to others, I found that my capacity to resist drinking grew stronger. Once I was focused and committed, I never wavered from wanting to be clean and stay clean. Neither should you. Be willing to put in the work so you can turn your hope into the reality you have planned for yourself. And make sure you hold yourself accountable along the way.

TROY AIKMAN

Don't let your inability to keep yourself accountable prevent you from attaining your aspirations. There is no better time than now, especially if you're young. Keep trying; be relentless, even when all is lost. Always keep in mind that there is hope.

My past client, Troy Aikman, understood the value of accountability better than anyone. The year was 1989, and the Dallas Cowboys had just limped through a miserable year and landed the first pick in the first round of the draft. The team was desperate for a shot in the arm, and their eyes were on the newest and shiniest draft prospect: my client, UCLA quarterback Troy Aikman. While Troy was leading his UCLA team through the Cotton Bowl, Dallas Cowboys team president Tex Schramm was whipping up "Aikmania Frenzy" in advance of the draft.

He went on a campaign to get all of Dallas excited about the newest recruit. Schramm had the wherewithal to recognize Troy as a game-changer, someone who would fit into the Dallas culture and give the fanbase hope. Troy had spent part of his childhood in Southern California but later moved to Oklahoma. He shared many similar qualities with the Dallas community, such as his love of hunting and country music. In Schramm's eyes, Troy was a player that fans could cheer for on the field and relate to off the field. In that same year, Arkansas multimillionaire Jerry Jones purchased the Cowboys. His first move was to fire Schramm, super scout Gil Brandt, and the team's iconic head coach, Tom Landry. These were not popular moves. It didn't help that Jones had played football at the University of Arkansas, which made him an outsider.

Jones then hired coach Jimmy Johnson, who had just won the national championship at the University of Miami. It was a time of upheaval, with hope that Aikman's addition could provide some stability and star power for the rebuilt franchise. The Cowboys were still excited to welcome Troy with open arms, so much so that they invited us down to their headquarters in Valley Ranch for a meeting. They spent hours reiterating just how much they loved Troy and how they planned to build the entire franchise around him.

As the meeting dragged on, our stomachs growled with hunger, and we moved to the kitchen, where Jimmy Johnson served microwaved popcorn. At around midnight, Jerry and I adjourned to the lobby of the Grand Hyatt at the airport and talked all night. I emphasized the fact that the Cowboys could be the most valuable entertainment franchise in the world. The NFL was burgeoning:

pro football wasn't just a sport anymore; it was a multibillion-dollar entertainment empire. I said that agents and teams were looking at their relationships the wrong way.

The real battle was never labor vs management. Heavily publicized contract battles between players and management just push fans away. And collective bargaining negotiations that pitted millionaires against billionaires were unpalatable. Instead, I argued, owners, players, and their agents should focus on a shared goal: collectively exploding revenue. What is the best way to exponentially increase television revenue? What is the best way to build new stadiums that have naming rights, luxury boxes, premium seating, and high-tech scoreboards? How could we turbocharge the production and marketing of memorabilia? We needed a way for everyone to receive a piece of the pie without working independently.

Unlike the traditional owner who had a limited sense of what was possible, Jerry was so bright, so creative, and so open to new ideas that I left the meeting thinking this was the owner who would take football into a new frontier of profitability. The Cowboys made Troy the first overall pick in the 1989 draft. In 1989, players still had to finish all four years of eligibility before they could declare for the NFL draft, a rule that was changed the following year. An exception to this rule was made for certain players who were ready to declare despite a few technicalities. These players did not go through the normal draft; instead, the NFL created the supplemental draft for them, and, as in the NFL draft, the Cowboys had the first pick.

But there was a hitch in the plan. Aikman was not the only heir apparent. During Johnson's time at the University of Miami, he won a national title thanks to his quarterback, Steve Walsh. Walsh declared for the supplemental draft, and four months after Troy signed, Walsh was added to the Dallas Cowboys' roster as another quarterback.

Talk about an unexpected shock for Troy. He'd been promised the full support of his team and coach and time to develop—but in an instant, that all changed. He didn't have the same relationship with Johnson that Walsh did, and this only added unnecessary pressure. Now, on top of adjusting to the blistering speed and complex defenses of the NFL, Troy had a quarterback controversy on his hands. It was a challenging situation and raised the stakes for Troy. A pick-six or an ill-timed sack that lost a game would threaten the momentum of a budding career. I thought of Troy when I first walked into sober living. I had all these obstacles up against me, and they just seemed to keep piling on. Quitting would've been the easy route for both Troy and me, but we owed it to ourselves to keep fighting. We had declared our goals, and we were going to keep at them—no excuses. The only thing Troy could do was to stay in the process and do his best.

Troy won the starting role in the preseason, but his trials were just beginning. Troy had to find the internal strength to prepare for what would be a torturous first year. The Cowboys lost the first eleven games. The running joke among the fans was that, if Jones purchased the 7-Eleven franchise, he'd have to rename it the 0/11. Game after game, Troy was getting sacked and pounded because he didn't have a supportive team. By the time that miserable season ended, he had thrown twice as many interceptions as touchdowns.

At this point, Troy and I were having multiple conversations about his future. I asked Troy, "Are you frustrated enough to think about getting traded to a team that really needs you?" No one disputed that he was the best quarterback in his draft class. Other teams would surely fulfill the promise Dallas had made. Then I asked him if he liked living in Dallas.

He responded, "I love it."

I asked him if he thought Jerry Jones was brilliant and would do anything to win. Troy agreed. Then I asked if he thought Head Coach Jimmy Johnson was uniquely gifted to coach him, and he again responded yes.

"So, let's think of the Cowboys as a finely tuned computer that simply didn't have enough memory," I said. Troy decided to continue striving. He was bright enough to understand that the conundrum he was in was only temporary. He reasoned that Dallas was the perfect place for him and that, eventually, with enough experience and information, Jimmy Johnson and Jerry Jones would get it right. To Troy, it was worth living through that miserable first year and enduring a couple of rough seasons to reach the promised land.

Like my client June, he used the power of his self-will to see beyond his current circumstance. He held himself accountable to the process. The following year, his patience and resiliency paid off. The Cowboys traded Walsh to the New Orleans Saints and drafted another infusion of great athletes, including Hall of Fame running back Emmitt Smith.

By 1992, the Cowboys were loaded with talent and competed in the 1993 Super Bowl at the Rose Bowl in Pasadena, California. As the Blue Angels roared in the skies above during the pregame show, Troy told me he had a hard time catching his breath; he couldn't believe he was beginning to see the light at the end of the tunnel. That day, the Cowboys dominated the Buffalo Bills 52-17, and Troy was selected MVP. En route to the team hotel in Santa Monica, I asked Troy if he understood what just happened.

He looked at me and said, "Yes, we just won the game."

"No," I said. "It is more than that. You entered the game as 'Troy Aikman,' a very good quarterback, and you are leaving the game as 'TROY AIKMAN SUPERSTAR.' Your life will never be the same, Troy."

He looked at me skeptically again.

When we arrived at the hotel, a massive crowd of ecstatic Cowboys fans had swarmed the entrance, and they went into hysterics when they saw Troy. We needed security to help escort us from the car door to the hotel. The next morning, Troy appeared on the Today Show, Good Morning America, and the CBS Morning News, and that night on Jay

Leno's Tonight Show. Within a day, he had become a household name. The Cowboys are known as "America's team," and Troy had become America's quarterback.

Troy went on to lead the Cowboys to the Super Bowl in 1994 and again in 1996. Troy had a responsibility to see his dream through, and even when everyone doubted his plan, he kept on his path. I'm glad Troy stuck to his guns and played out his career in Dallas. I would hate to see how things might have ended up if he had requested a trade. Sometimes the player has to guide the agent.

Accountability means staying the course and seeing things through. But it doesn't necessarily mean keeping the same attitude. Sometimes you need a mental shift to stick to the plan. Oprah Winfrey once said, "The greatest discovery of all time is that a person can change his future by merely changing his attitude." To honor my responsibility to my comeback as a sports agent, I needed to change my mentality. Troy clung to his vision of a brighter tomorrow, and I needed to do the same. If Troy could withstand his first couple of years as a Dallas Cowboy, then I could endure sober living. I just needed to make sure I committed to it the way Troy did with the Cowboys.

And like the way the Cowboys organization stood behind Troy during the bad years, I knew sober living had my back the same way. Being accountable to your dreams is no easy feat, especially when other occupational endeavors offer an easier route. Sometimes it feels like you're standing alone on a hill, while everyone is advising you to let go of the dream and move on to something else. Something more attainable. But it's something that doesn't ignite your passions. Ignore these "voices of reason," for they are not reasonable at all.

As time passed, I began to adjust to my new life at sober living. After joining the house and interacting with the people there, I was comfortable with myself, and I finally realized what was needed to reestablish sobriety. I understood I had to own up to past indiscretions and faithfully fulfill the promises I made to myself and to others to change my behavior. Certainly, accountability can be humbling; it forces you to reckon with your weaknesses, as well as your strengths. But being accountable means putting your ego aside. Once I vowed to take responsibility for my actions, my future seemed brighter and long-term sobriety seemed more attainable than ever.

TAYLOR HEINICKE

There were times when I felt like the mythical Greek figure Sisyphus, who was doomed for all eternity to spend each day pushing a boulder up a hill, only for it to roll back down again. When you're in crisis, the dark days sometimes seem like they are never going to end. In such moments, perseverance is harder than ever—it's also more important than ever. Taylor Heinicke embodied this lesson.

Taylor was a quarterback out of Old Dominion University in Virginia. His dazzling talent was somewhat undercut by his size, standing six feet tall rather than 6'3" or 6'4" like most quarterbacks in the league. He signed with Steinberg Sports out of college, but he wasn't selected in the 2015 draft. Instead, our firm signed him as an undrafted free agent with the Minnesota Vikings. This was just the beginning of a long and draining odyssey of being tossed from team to team. In 2017, he was signed to the New England Patriots practice squad, only to be released two months later. In a span of two years, he joined the Houston Texans, the Carolina Panthers, and finally the St. Louis Battle Hawks in the XFL.

Most people think the lives of professional athletes are just one thrill after another, but few understand how grueling it is to compete in any professional sport. And the career of a journeyman like Taylor embodies that: it's hard to bounce from team to team, always on the edge of being released or traded, never sure if you'll have a job next season.

The grind to success in the NFL is one of the toughest. And being a quarterback is at the pinnacle of hard. Meanwhile, you can't complain or take your foot off the gas. In all those moves, Taylor had to learn each team's playbook, execute what he learned, and stay upbeat every minute to let the organization know he was their guy and they should keep him.

In 2019, tired and beaten down, Taylor had reached a fork in the road. Players in this position, bouncing from team to team on short-term contracts and having failed to really gain a foothold in the league, begin to question whether the dream is still worth pursuing. Should he salvage his losses now and start the next phase of life, or give it yet one last shot? There's an old saying: "The moment you give up on your dream is the moment your opportunity arrives."

It is akin to a person in the desert trekking across the sand with no sight of water and giving up when he gets within a hundred meters of the oasis. That said, as nice as the sentiment is, some people just don't make it, no matter how stubbornly they refuse to give in. Success and longevity are by no means guaranteed. Taylor had finished college in 2015 and, four years later, around the time NFL QBs were entering their prime, he was in a minor league making virtually no income. He could either press on and try to return to the NFL or throw in the towel.

Taylor picked up the football and took a Hail Mary shot to the end zone. In December of 2020, he caught a break and signed with the Washington Commanders' practice squad (then called the Washington Football Team). He wasn't the starting quarterback, and he barely made the team, but when the Commanders' starter, Ryan Fitzpatrick, got injured, he was put into the game. Finally! He had a chance to show his game, and Taylor wasn't going to waste the opportunity. He thrived in the relief role and led his team to a victory against the Giants the following week. As the season went on, he continued to make a name for himself by proving himself an effective player.

Despite his best efforts, though, the Commanders made a trade for Carson Wentz to be the new starting quarterback for the 2022 season. There were doubters within the Washington organization who asserted that Taylor was too short and that his arm was not strong enough, so the trade made perfect sense. Carson Wentz had been the second pick overall in the 2016 draft. He had been the franchise quarterback for the Philadelphia Eagles and the Indianapolis Colts. Everyone in the media said Wentz had the better upside and future potential to be Washington's starting quarterback.

Ultimately, this move sent Taylor back to the bench. Now the question on Taylor's mind was what more did he have to do to show people his talent? He played well in 2021, but that still wasn't enough. He was at another crossroads: persevere by enduring overlooked roles out of the spotlight, or move on to something else? Those who persevere and stay committed to the journey are often rewarded with what may seem like lucky breaks. In truth, perseverance isn't about waiting for good things to happen—it's about pushing forward, preparing, and being ready to rise when opportunity presents itself.

So, when Wentz fractured his ring finger, Taylor headed to the field yet again, and he was back with a vengeance. He went on a winning streak, once more proving that he deserved the starting position. The marginal QB who had been cut over and over again showed the world that his resolve was indomitable and his belief in himself was steadfast. There will be a better tomorrow if you have a plan and continue working to execute it.

He started in 2022 and, after winning a few games, he was declared the starter. It didn't even matter if Wentz came back from the injury; Washington was finally sticking with Taylor.

Taylor had something I had, too: the backing of a supportive team. When I was at sober living, I didn't have to summit that mountain alone. The other guys were there to hold me to account and motivate me, not to mention the dedicated professionals who devote their lives to helping people achieve and maintain sobriety. Taylor was well-liked by the other Washington players. That, in turn, empowered him to keep his eye on the ball, so to speak—on the dream that had motivated him since he was a kid.

Given what Taylor endured, an ordinary person would have given up and gotten a regular nine-to-five job. Taylor, on the other hand, had the self-confidence and religious faith to look beyond the current circumstances and feel confident that everything would work out okay. He was traded from the Atlanta Falcons to the Los Angeles Chargers at the beginning of the 2024 NFL season. But he's proven to everyone—and most importantly, to himself—that he's got the skill, determination, and self-accountability to hold his own as a starter and build a long, admirable career in the toughest league in the world. And that in and of itself is a great victory—and as good a comeback story as any.

Chapter 7

Relationships: Someone to Lean On

As I've shared before, one of the deepest wounds left by my alcoholism was the strain it placed on my relationships, especially with family. That pain ran deep, as I had been raised to cherish family above all else. Relationships are the foundation of life, but in sobriety, they become even more sacred. No battle, especially the battle for sobriety, is meant to be fought alone. A comeback journey is rarely a solo endeavor. Mountaineers who climb Everest can't do it without their sherpa.

And in all the examples of athletic redemption I talk about in this book, those players had coaches, teammates, and family members supporting them along the way, often quietly, out of the spotlight. Through mentorship, active listening, and self-reflection, I began to rebuild what had been broken. These tools became the compass that guided me toward many days on the sunny side of the street.

MENTORSHIP

Sober living gave me the structure and routine I needed, and the environment to essentially make sobriety my full-time job. I lived there from March 2010 to December 2010 and, during that time, I had a single-minded focus on one thing: quitting drinking once and for all. In the past, I had come out of rehab telling everyone I knew that this time, "I got it. This time is going to be different." But it never worked.

So, at sober living, I refrained from sharing with outside friends and family what was going on. They didn't want to hear it. They wanted to see my actions. All anyone cared about was the number of days of sobriety I had maintained.

Previously, during my other attempts to quit, I was never truly anonymous. Men like to talk about sports. Men who recognized me or knew my line of work would ask me questions about my clients. One day, someone approached me in the bathroom with a DVD of Jerry Maguire and asked me to autograph it. As much as I tried to be gracious and welcoming, this attention distracted me from what was important. I needed a safe group that would allow me to be an anonymous, humble alcoholic searching for solutions just like everybody else. In my home group, there was little recognition of who I was in the world. For one, inside the house, everyone was equal. For another, most of the other guys were not all that interested in pro sports. They were spending their free time camping, bungee jumping, fixing up motorcycles, planning their next dirt bike excursion, or thinking about their next tattoo. My home group allowed me to work on my problems rather than be a celebrity.

And in the house, I could avail myself of an invaluable resource: the wisdom of fellow alcoholics. In the group home, I realized that, for most of my life, I had held the position "expert." We are all experts at something or another. Maybe you are the best singer, artist, or cook who gives relatives the best tips and tricks to cook a wood-fired pizza. Maybe you are the handiest and can fix any motor or electronic device. Perhaps you're an exceptional writer, constantly editing and revising others' work. I was an expert on the challenges that young athletes face. My natural role was giving life advice to my friends, family, and clients. I was always the repository of wisdom.

But admitting to myself that I wasn't in control of my alcoholism also made me aware that there was a lot about behavior and psychology I didn't know. To achieve sobriety, I needed to shed the role of teacher/counselor and learn everything I could about recovery from others. There is a popular saying in the business world: "If you're the smartest person in the room, you need to find another room." You learn from the brilliance of those who surround you; they lift you. To advance your knowledge, you want to surround yourself with people who have more expertise in areas you haven't mastered.

Our minds need to be stimulated to grow. If no one in the room is challenging you or adding to your knowledge space, then you know that's the wrong room for you. And listening and learning from the elders only validated that. It was an odd feeling for me, but I knew they were going to help me get back on the right path, and that's exactly what they did. Now that I had fully committed myself to recovery, I felt like I had gone back to college, for more reasons than one. It was as if I was back in a lecture hall listening to a professor. During the home group meetings, I'd find everyone who had achieved long-term sobriety and listen as they shared. I didn't attempt to jump into the conversation—beyond asking a question or two, I just listened. At first, it was hard not to be involved in the conversation. I had made a fortune by shaping the narrative in every room, using the gift of persuasion and cultivating expertise in matters people paid top dollar for. But once I quickly realized that I had no clue how to beat my addiction alone, I enthusiastically accepted the lessons the old timers were teaching and tried to become an A student in their program. Books, ears, and eyes were all open and ready to absorb.

There was also a social atmosphere in the house that reminded me of my college days. There was a strong sense of camaraderie and lots of laughter. Just because we were serious about getting sober didn't mean there wasn't room for levity.

My home group, which I joined, was an all-male group, called "a stag," of people working the Twelve Steps. When I first walked into the room, it looked like a cross between a tattoo parlor, the cast of Pirates of the Caribbean, and a gathering of the Hell's Angels. I wasn't amongst my normal peers, but they quickly became a cherished support group. Over time, they would become like family.

Amongst our differences, I discovered our similarities. And within those similarities, we found common ground that would be the foundation for lasting relationships. At the end of the day, we were like soldiers, thrown together from different walks of life and called upon to fight in a war that was, for many of us, a matter of life and death. I owe those men a deep debt that I can only repay by helping others who are struggling.

Listening to the men at my home group gave me hope and inspired me. It didn't matter your background. What mattered was us supporting each other so that we all would win. In my past experiences in rehabs, it was about each person individually winning. It was challenging to build genuine relationships at those rehab centers because the patients kept coming and going. Now, I felt like I was part of a group that was committed to keeping each other sober and staying together. During that year, I watched these men in my home group deal with the death of a child, cancer, loss of a parent, hospitalization, and a variety of other tragedies. They were able to get through these situations without any liquid crutch, and it inspired me to achieve sobriety alongside them.

My struggle became my group's struggle and vice versa. We opened up and shared uncomfortable feelings and difficult memories with each other. We exchanged intimate stories about our past failings and our future goals. We kept each other accountable. They helped me put my recovery plan in motion.

It wasn't just the emotional and philosophical discussions that were edifying, but the practical life tips, too. Lounging in the living room, or out back in the sunny yard amidst the lemon trees, we passed around advice about what had worked for us to resist cravings and avoid drinking—how to actually put the Twelve Steps into practice, day by day.

For example, my mentor Chip G. taught me the acronym HALT, which refers to everyday needs (Hunger, Anger, Loneliness, and Tired) that can induce an alcoholic to drink. Rather than using alcohol to sate discomfort, HALT reminds us to give our body what it is asking for. If I'm hungry, I should eat. If I'm angry, I should go for a walk. When I feel lonely, I should look for a friend. And when I'm tired, I should sleep. HALT is a way for you to check in periodically with yourself to regulate and maintain healthy coping mechanisms that help you fight off problems when they surface, rather than letting them pile up like a stack of old books. In our early stages of sobriety, these check-ins are vital for self-care and improving our awareness. I'll admit it was intimidating at first. There is no precedent for living in a group home of alcoholics. I had been catapulted far outside of my comfort zone, but it's where I found sobriety.

Looking back, I'm grateful that Charle Street didn't have a bed prepared for me, because I wouldn't have met the men at sober living, men who changed my life forever. For example, Tom was an attorney who could talk about anything and everything. We bonded, and he became a kindred spirit. He had a calming, soothing presence and a quick wit, qualities that helped assuage my discomfort when the going got tough. We spent hours talking about our lives, our sobriety journeys, and our hopes for the future. He remains an indispensable pillar of support to this day.

Then there was my sponsor, Dwight. He is a musician and a construction worker who operates heavy machinery, so it might seem that we have little in common. Dwight jokingly referred to himself as a ditch digger, but he had great depths of wisdom, an encyclopedic knowledge of current affairs, and could quote Shakespeare. He was low-key and steady. He was a consistent source of wisdom and encouragement at our group meetings, and he constantly motivated me. But what really bonded us together was his mastery of the literature and the traditions of the Twelve-Step program. I absorbed so much from him.

Kevin was another confidante: a 6'4" former pro basketball player with a booming voice and larger-than-life personality. Kevin would conduct the weekly meetings, where I learned so much about how to apply the Twelve Steps to my daily life and why I had failed before.

One of my greatest mentors happened to be the woman of my dreams, Amy Stoody. She is a brilliant trial lawyer with long-term sobriety. Amy is funny, high-spirited, empathetic, and always a good sport, all qualities I value greatly. We bonded over our mutual love of travel, books, movies, the beach, people, and politics. She is also drop-dead gorgeous, not to mention. But there was one fracture point between us: I was drinking, and she wasn't. When I could keep it together, things went well, but my habit created friction. Before sober living, she begged me to get sober, which I wanted more than anything. I just couldn't do it.

Amy really was the love of my life. I thought we were on the road to marriage. But it all came crashing down when she drove one evening to my mother's house, where I had been staying. We sat in the living room, and she took me by the hand. "This isn't working for me. I can't help you. You have to face this alone. I can't be codependent. I love you, but I can't live like this." That was the final, vertiginous descent to a real bottom. In retrospect, breaking up with me was the kindest and most constructive gift she could have given me because, shortly thereafter, I entered into the sober living house. It was devastating, but probably what I needed the most.

ACTIVE LISTENING

In a chapter on the importance of relationships to your comeback, I need to address communication and listening. Communication is the lifeblood of all relationships: personal, professional, social, and familial. Yet the art of communication is often lost on people, and that no doubt contributes to the erosion of the relationships they need to lift them. Usually, this is because it is one-sided. People are keen to talk, less keen to listen. In reality, the key to communication is listening to others and working through the misunderstandings that can arise. Don't be so quick to formulate your argument or response while the other is talking. Just listen. Active listening helps draw another person out in discussion and move beyond surface responses. By asking another person to identify their priorities and values, you can dive deeper into the ability to put yourself in someone else's heart and mind.

When was the last time you truly listened to someone? Sat down to lend your ear rather than your voice? Active listening skills are the secret ingredient to connectivity, accountability, and healing. Somehow, I had lost my capacity for active listening. And in doing so, I was tuning out the words and wisdom of others—people who had my back and wanted me to succeed.

Finally, at sober living, I was getting it back. It's humbling if you're used to being the talker, the most impactful voice in the room, the go-to expert, or the one with all the charisma. Listening is challenging, especially during a comeback. Especially when the words you might be hearing echo the painful truth you've been attempting to hide from. It's easier to fill a room with your breath than admit when you're wrong.

Active listening is a tool that builds and strengthens relationships at every step. Regardless of how uncomfortable it made me, I had to listen to recover, redeem myself, and give others confidence in my comeback. Understanding other people's perspectives and hurt, though painful to hear, opened my eyes to the damage I had caused.

By relying on my active listening skills, I'd created a community of friends and clients I could depend on, and they could rely on me. In our interactions, I tried to address them uniquely, getting into their hearts and minds to create a clearer picture of what life was like in their shoes. They reciprocated the kindness, and thus we enjoyed spending time together because we took the time to listen to one another. Our relationships blossomed and strengthened with each interaction.

This may be one of the most complex tools to master because listening requires accountability, selflessness, transparency, and humility. The responsibility to yourself and to those you've hurt along the way is critical for you to accept. Making amends is hard to do unless you have done the work beforehand. Be selfless and transparent enough to accept the truth rather than try to outweigh it with your voice.

During your journey, no matter how hard you try to hide what's really going on in your life, people will see right through it. Not everyone, but the ones who know you best. They remember the authentic person you used to be and will turn their back on you again if you appear to be a fraud in their eyes. Hear them and they will hear you. One day, I got an unexpected call from someone I hadn't spoken to in some time: my son. If there ever was a time to hush up and listen, this was it.

"Dad, I'd like you to come to my graduation." He was finishing film school a year early.

"I'd be happy to come," I said, getting emotional. "I'm really proud of you."

"Cool. I'll let you know the details," he said. And that was it—the great thawing of a once-loving relationship turned icy. That day, we didn't mention our estrangement. We didn't talk about "the issues." We didn't have to. There was damage to repair, amends to make, but that could come later. Instead, there was great power in what was left unsaid, and in the space between words, I knew this invitation meant, "Dad, I want you back in my life."

As the year went on and the number of days sober stacked up, other family members were beginning to see a change in me. My brother Jim was proud of me. I had put Jim through a lot with my drinking. It's painful to watch someone you love self-destruct in slow motion. But he never faltered, never wavered, and never left me to my own devices. It was Jim who helped get me into rehab the first few times. And when rehab didn't work, Jim was the one who drove me to Charle Street and stayed by my side when they turned me away and we had to find an alternative.

Jim had faith in me that I would be redeemed, and I think knowing that, even on a subconscious level, strengthened my resolve. It helped that Jim is one of the few people who has known me my whole life. Because we grew up in the same household, with the same values, it was like we shared a secret code or a special language. Few people understand you as well as your siblings. And I know not everyone has a healthy relationship with their brothers and sisters. Still, your comeback is an opportunity to honor that relationship—to honor it by leaning on it. And if you're estranged from your brothers or sisters, maybe the comeback is a chance to repair those broken bonds.

That's the experience of many addicts, who alienate their family for a time but then reestablish that relationship when they achieve sobriety. As important as it is to build a community and learn from others, it's just as important to nurture and maintain that community. And that work starts from within. Before I could show up fully for others—family, friends, colleagues—I had to learn to face myself. The truth is, we can't give what we don't have. If I wanted to rebuild trust, restore broken relationships, and become the person others could depend on again, I had to look inward first. That's where self-reflection came in.

SELF-REFLECTION

The answer to most of life's questions is typically right in front of us. Most of us tend not to be honest with ourselves, even though we should be. I hear the phrase "I'm just keeping it real" a lot, but most people rarely keep it real about who they really are. We all tend to be guarded about people knowing things about us that we consider off-limits. But behind closed doors, there are no limits. No hiding, running, or lying. When you start reflecting on who you are, the truth will slowly begin to reveal itself. The beautiful thing about self-reflection is that it's you analyzing you. It's the best time to start correcting things wrong in your life and find solutions to fix them. The Berkeley Well-Being Institute defines self-reflection as "a mental process you can use to grow your understanding of who you are, what your values are, and why you think, feel, and act the way you do. When you self-reflect and become more conscious of what drives you, you can more easily make changes that help you to develop yourself or improve your life."

From self-reflection, I realized what I wanted my comeback to be: being a good father and making a difference in the world. Monetary aspects were much lower on the list of priorities. By looking at the following values and prioritizing them, you can define how to gauge your own comeback. You need to be clear about what you believe your role in life is. It is critical for individuals to take time to reflect on which values and priorities they consider most crucial. Taking the time to look ahead and see which elements in life are necessary to fulfill can help set you on the right path. If you're new to self-reflection, I suggest creating a questionnaire to clarify your goals. Here are some questions I recommend starting with. What are your plans for short-term financial gain? What about long-term financial security? What kind of geographical location would you like to live in? Do you have spiritual values? Do you crave personal autonomy—more control over your life, business, and how you spend your time? What kind of working conditions do you prefer—maybe you love working from home? Or perhaps you recognize you can do your best work in a corner office with big windows. How many vacation hours are you looking for? Do you genuinely believe in the business you are working for?

Prioritizing these constellations of values helps clarify your own goals or better understand someone else. I've used similar questionnaires with my clients, such as gifted Arizona Cardinals strong safety Tim McDonald.

When Tim McDonald became eligible for free agency in 1993, multiple franchises competed for his services. Tim had been a Pro Bowl safety with the Arizona Cardinals. When representing a free agent with numerous options, there needs to be self-reflection on the athlete's priorities. The question Tim had to figure out was where he wanted to play. We took a piece of paper and got to work.

We needed to figure out what he cared most about and in which order.

Was his top priority finding a quality coach? Maybe he wanted to find a team with an amazing defensive line. Or maybe he wanted a team with a proven head coach. By answering these questions, Tim prioritized being part of a winning team and staying close to family in Fresno, California. That's why signing with the San Francisco 49ers was an easy decision. They matched his top priorities.

The mental process of self-reflection isn't something that happens instantly or overnight. Instead, it takes practice. The more practice, the more you can use it in your life. Self-reflection is one key that can help you in your decision-making process—it can clarify your inner priorities. Not what the world thinks you should care about, but rather your own truth.

When dramatic or traumatic events occur in people's lives, it might take years until they have the mental willingness to revisit the moment and look at it with a critical point of view. What happened in this event, and how did it affect me? Were my actions warranted, or did I overreact? Sitting and reflecting can be hard because we risk that wave of emotions returning from the memory of the event. Rather than sitting with the pain, some want to sublimate their emotions and move on, unable to come to terms with their actions. Learn to forgive yourself because underlying those difficult emotions is a lesson waiting to be learned. Throughout this book, you will hear me return to the topic of self-reflection because it's an important tool in your day-to-day life. But in this day and age, achieving self-reflection seems like an impossible task with the number of distractions surrounding us. Younger people who have grown up in this high-tech environment have an especially hard time focusing.

Technology has the alluring power of escapism. The small, rectangular device in your pocket can literally transport you into another world where your reality doesn't exist. The recent technological advances can and should be celebrated, but one's dependency on them robs us of the time for self-reflection and the ability to face the current situation that we all need.

Chapter 8

Resilience: Never Stop Pushing

Nine months in sober living had given me the breakthrough I needed. I was now on my way to the next part of my comeback: rebuilding my business. I started going on talk radio shows, speaking on podcasts, and looking for other ways to reenter the sports world. But as news of my intentions to return as an agent got out, there were skeptics. The most prominent MLB agent was quoted as saying that my career had no chance of being resurrected.

Some people thought I was audacious for even trying. They had written me off. In particular, my competitors were unsupportive. It's a cutthroat business. Your comeback might not involve a business venture, but you will face naysayers, skeptics, and haters, especially if you have something others covet or are pursuing a goal others also desire. The very fact of your existence might be anathema to them. Certainly, there would be people who followed the development in the hopes that I would fall again.

Unfortunately, too many agents are ruthlessly competitive and, instead of embracing their peers, see fellow agents as adversaries. Since I had a high profile, my fall had been heavily publicized. In every newspaper headline, on every sports news channel globally, my missteps were broadcast. I never thought I was all that newsworthy, but the press loves a good scandal.

There's a lesson there: so far, I've talked about relationships in the context of restoring ones that have faltered and leaning on those that persist through the dark times, because you can't come back without the support of others. But draw strength from your cheerleaders and ignore your naysayers. There will be people who doubt you. Some doubters are acting in bad faith and do not have your best interests at heart; they may even want you to fail.

We have all come into contact with these people at some point in our lives. They seem harmless, but in many ways, they are jealous that you are doing something that they wish they could do or feel like they could do better than you. They will question the things you are doing and wait for the opportunity to rip it apart, giving you what they perceive as the right way to do it. Even in recovery, you meet these people disguised as friends questioning your treatment, even to the point of saying you can recover without it. In life, you have to surround yourself with people who are supportive and will believe in your dreams. You have to stay strong and committed and, regardless of what others say around you, remember to own the recovery and the path that you are on.

Tune them out and stick to your journey. Resilience requires looking forward, with a clear-eyed focus on the goal. It won't be easy but stay true to yourself and believe in your comeback. Regardless of your age, we all need a friend in a comeback story. Sometimes that's a mentor: someone who shows you the way, probably because they've walked it, too. Sometimes it's a friend: a sympathetic ear, a shoulder to cry on, an unwavering source of emotional support and encouragement.

Like most things, a comeback cannot be done alone; it takes a village. If you don't have one now, start building it up. Your village doesn't have to be populated with people like you; in fact, there is a missed opportunity in only consorting with those who share your background. You never know who might change your life. One constant source of inspiration during my planning for my return was the example of one of my earliest clients, Rolf Benirschke.

ROLF BENIRSCHKE

Rolf Benirschke was a serious zoology major at UC Davis and an outstanding placekicker, coached by the legendary Jim Sochor. His off-the-field charm matched his talents on the gridiron. Rolf was handsome and intelligent, with a warm and engaging personality. When I was young and new to the world of athletic representation, Rolf and I quickly developed a friendship that transcended the stereotypical agent-player relationship and led to many special shared memories.

If not for a technicality, he would have been the last player picked in the 1977 NFL Draft, which would have granted him the tongue-in-cheek honor of being "Mr. Irrelevant." Mr. Irrelevant was annually recognized at a Newport Beach banquet along with a golf tournament and a week of festivities, lauding his status as the last player picked in the draft. Every year at the banquet I was asked to play the role of surrogate agent for this player, negotiating a fanciful blockbuster contract that had the same worth as the paper it was printed on. The contract included a clause stating that "the Player didn't have to play in a game where the temperature dropped below fifty degrees." It also had a clause that "the player did not have to practice on any day that ended with the letter 'Y.'" The contract was a joke because nobody ever believed the last pick would actually make a team! That concept changed over time when Brock Purdy became a fifty-million-per-year quarterback for the San Francisco 49ers in 2022. And three years later, Purdy signed a five-year, $265-million contract extension with the 49ers, with $181 million in guaranteed money. Talk about rewriting the legacy of Mr. Irrelevant—he went from an afterthought to the face of one of the NFL's most storied franchises.

Rolf was released by the Raiders (again over a technicality) and claimed by his hometown team, the San Diego Chargers. At least he had family nearby. Several years before, Rolf's father Kurt had been recruited to join the new med school at UC San Diego as the Chairman of Pathology and uprooted the family from their comfortable East Coast roots at Dartmouth College. While Kurt was a medical doctor, he was also fascinated by the world-renowned San

Diego Zoo and the possibility of applying scientific and medical knowledge to help save endangered animals. He was allowed to establish a research center called CRES, the Center for Reproduction of Endangered Species, where Rolf worked during his summers while home from college.

As a player in the NFL (even an "irrelevant" one), it didn't take long for Rolf to recognize he had been given a unique platform, and that he could use it to direct attention to things he really believed in. One of those passions was the plight of endangered species. After lots of discussion, we came up with the idea of a matching charitable challenge called "Kicks for Kritters" that we rolled out in San Diego. For every field goal Rolf kicked during the season, he would donate fifty dollars to the program and encourage Chargers fans to join him. Remember, this was 1977, when players didn't make much money, and fifty bucks had a lot more purchasing power.

We then produced a poster with pledge cards attached and placed them in all kinds of bars, restaurants, and other businesses that cherished the very popular Chargers. If someone walked into a 7-Eleven or a bank in San Diego in those days, they would see these posters and pledge cards and could easily get involved. The first poster showed him kicking a field goal while a sea lion's flipper held the ball. The following year, it was teed up by a baby elephant's foot. The campaign worked. Soon, business leaders were giving $1,000 for each field goal, and kids were giving twenty-five cents.

We then assembled an advisory board that included Mayor Pete Wilson, Chief of Police Bill Kolendar, and other business and community leaders. Rolf began working with local grade schools and junior high schools, and developed "Cans for Critters," an educational and fundraising program that was embraced by dozens of schools. The program not only raised public understanding of endangered species but also contributed key funding to the zoo's ongoing research. Over the course of Rolf's ten-year career, more than two million dollars was raised to help preserve species in peril and, to this day, he runs into people who remind him of when he came to their school to talk about endangered animals when they were in the fourth or fifth grade way back in the 1980s! This is a pure example of an athlete as a role model and community figure.

It was a promising start to a career, but in his second season, he started to develop intense abdominal pain and his weight dropped dramatically. He was diagnosed with Crohn's Disease, and his illness was played out publicly as the whole community empathized with his struggle.

One day, midway through his third season, he collapsed on the team plane while flying home from a game against New England and was immediately taken to a hospital in San Diego for emergency surgery. He required a second surgery six days later, contracting sepsis in the process and sparking fears for his survival. Would he live or would he die? No one knew.

Rolf's second operation left him weighing 123 pounds, more than sixty pounds below his playing weight, with an ostomy bag attached to his side to collect his waste. At just twenty-four years of age, this was a life-altering moment. Not only was he sure his football career was over, but he wondered if life was even worth fighting for at all. But Rolf kept fighting. Rooted deeply in his Christian faith, he trusted wholeheartedly that God would carry him through and never forsake him.

He also had the support of a loving family, friends, teammates, and a community that rallied around him. He was encouraged to read some of the books written by POW survivors who had endured terrible circumstances in the camps where they were held and applied some of the practices they shared to his own situation. He figured if it could work for POWs who fought to survive each day and never gave up hope of being liberated, it could work for him.

He learned to break time down into bite-sized pieces, one day at a time, to set small, daily goals so the enormity of the challenge he was facing didn't overwhelm him. In the process, like the POWs he had read about, he discovered things about himself he didn't previously appreciate. He learned he had more courage, greater perseverance, and more patience and creativity than he ever imagined. Today, he would tell you he wouldn't trade that extraordinarily difficult time for anything, because it shaped him into the man he is today. It made him resilient. And when you are resilient, you can bear any burden. Not only did Rolf live, but he achieved what he had thought was impossible: he returned to football.

There is an iconic picture of huge defensive tackle Louie Kelcher walking a frail Rolf onto the field at the stadium for the pregame coin toss. At the time, Rolf would tell you that he figured this would be the last time he would ever be on the field as a Charger. But somehow, remarkably, Rolf recovered and played seven more seasons, providing many more thrills for Chargers fans. It wasn't easy, though, and required intense medical intervention. For example, he had to undergo another surgery just to move his ostomy bag so he could kick better. But he was determined. This was his dream. And nothing was going to stop him.

When Rolf left the game after ten years, he remained very involved in the San Diego community. He founded the Legacy Invitational Golf Tournament, which is still played today, sits on the Board of the San Diego Zoo and several other non-profits, and founded a patient engagement company that works with many major pharmaceutical and medical device companies. Recently, he helped fund and put together a biotechnology company that was sold to Merck. This company will soon be bringing new treatments to market to help fellow IBD sufferers. He will tell you that he is truly the most grateful patient you will ever meet!

Few comeback stories are as inspiring or dramatic as Rolf's—literally on the brink of death, he mustered the will to fight back against his illness, restore his health, and make an unlikely return to a highly competitive, physically grueling league.

WARREN MOON

No one understands you like you do. I couldn't let others' doubts about me stop me from reaching my goals, and no one understood this more than my friend and client for nineteen years, Warren Moon. Before Warren Moon became a record-breaking quarterback and Hall of Fame athlete, he was just a young man who wanted more than anything to play football in the NFL. He attended Alexander Hamilton High School in Los Angeles, which was my alma mater, so we instantly bonded when we met later, in 1977.

At the time, there had been only a handful of Black quarterbacks in the league, because some in the NFL held the unspoken notion that African Americans lacked the intellectual capacity to play quarterback. It is hard to imagine a past like that, given the current dominance of Black quarterbacks in the NFL.

In his first two years as a starter at the University of Washington, his team went 11-11, but despite the middling record, Warren exhibited qualities that would later earn him a spot in the NFL. He was a gifted athlete with charisma and a first-rate intellect. He had precision passing skills. By his senior year, Warren led his team to a surprise upset in the 1978 Rose Bowl over the heavily favored Michigan. He was also named co-MVP in the PAC-8.

He fit the definition of a quarterback to a tee, but when he declared his intent to head to the draft in that position, he was met with extreme doubt and criticism. Many NFL scouts told us we should encourage him to switch to running back or wide receiver. But he stuck to his guns. I asked Warren what his feelings were about a position switch. He responded, "Never. I was born to play quarterback." Given the widespread (and racist) skepticism of him, we expected that he would be selected in the lower rounds in the draft, which would have relegated him to a backup role. He wanted to start and play as soon as possible, though. So, we turned our sights to other opportunities. Six weeks prior to the draft, Warren signed with the Edmonton Eskimos in the Canadian Football League, and he was a star.

As a quarterback, Warren led his team to five consecutive Grey Cup victories, which was Canada's version of the Super Bowl. He earned the Grey Cup MVP title twice, earned the CFL's Most Outstanding Player award and became the first professional quarterback in the CFL to pass for 5,000 yards in his final year. Warren had to learn to believe in himself and tune out the outside noise. Instead of allowing their doubt to make him question himself, he went into another league to prove everyone wrong.

One off-season, we attended a Super Bowl game at the Rose Bowl in Pasadena. It was like watching a sick kid at home, pressing his face against the living room window, enviously watching his friends play outside. I could sense his longing to return to the US and play quarterback in the NFL, and soon his prayers were answered.

We timed Warren's contract so that, after six years in Canada, he would be a free agent with the option to play in one of three leagues: the Canadian Football League, the National Football League, or the fledgling United States Football League. Because he hadn't been drafted in the NFL, he was an outlier in a restrictive system. He was a pure free agent in his prime, able to choose. Twelve teams in three different leagues expressed interest in speaking with him about his future. Suddenly, he found himself in the middle of a bidding war. A team could add the most critical position, quarterback, without giving up anything in return except his contract. Multiple franchises wanted Warren under center. Several owners, team executives, and head coaches pulled out all the stops to get him.

It made big national news when he signed with the Houston Oilers for $5.5 million, which set a new standard for NFL compensation. He went on to play for the Minnesota Vikings, Seattle Seahawks, and the Kansas City Chiefs. In his career, Warren ended up throwing for 70,553 yards and 435 touchdowns in total. Combining his totals from the CFL and NFL, he retired as the player with the most yards and touchdowns ever to play quarterback.

The greatest honor of my career was giving the induction speech as Warren became the first African American quarterback in the modern era to be inducted into the Pro Football Hall of Fame. He was also inducted into the Canadian Hall of Fame. To everyone else, Warren's story might seem like a marvel, but Warren always knew where he was heading. He could have easily changed his position and given up his dream of becoming an NFL quarterback, but he remained resolute. Perseverance and belief in your destiny will carry you through the fire and help preserve your faith in yourself.

As I exited sober living, various people and companies began approaching me, wanting to know if I was planning on getting back into representation. To them, I was a distressed brand they could buy at a discount, with the potential for an extremely high upside. Before I could provide an answer, though, I had to make a decision. Was I going to leave the agency behind or pick up where I left off? Leave the sports world behind and jump into a humanitarian career where I could focus on matters like civil rights, climate change, and other social issues? If you were to ask my college buddies what I'd be doing now, they'd have predicted I'd be a senator on Capitol Hill.

While considering my next moves, I reached out to Warren for his opinion. "Are you sure you want to get back into agenting?" he asked me. "Why not move on to your other passions? You've represented over sixty first-round draft picks, the first pick overall eight times, twelve players in the Pro Football Hall of Fame, and all the top baseball

players and boxers. No one else is ever going to replicate those numbers, so aren't you just competing against yourself?" I remember him asking these questions as if it were yesterday. His doubt paralleled my own questions: "Shouldn't you be working on books, movies, and setting up public speaking events? Helping establish charities and finding ways to give back to the community?"

Warren challenged me as to why I'd go back to something I'd already mastered. Maybe it was time to try something new. I thought back to being a kid, sitting around the dinner table with my parents and siblings. Every night, it was drilled into our heads that our purpose on this earth was to make a difference in the world. Could I do that as a sports agent?

I wrestled with this thought: no one would ever label running a sports agency as humanitarian work. And yet, I came to realize that the world of sports carries immense influence. By embracing that platform, I could unite my philanthropic passions with the business of athlete representation. It is a source of enormous wealth that can be channeled into charitable causes. Athletes and coaches are exalted as leaders and wield significant influence, both on a national scale and within their communities. Sports attract major players in the adjacent worlds of business, finance, and government—movers and shakers who can do good in the world, if they're encouraged to.

It became clear to me that, while I could begin anew in a traditional humanitarian or public-interest career, my greatest impact would come from leveraging what I knew best—being an agent—and channeling it toward a purpose that extended far beyond the playing field. I could achieve a much greater impact by harnessing the power of athletes, investors, and other sporting bigwigs than I could on my own.

As an agent, I could shape athletes into role models who used their platforms to better their communities. As an agent, I could finance and support a multitude of charities and other organizations. As an agent, I could bring my father's lessons to a broader audience. My mind was made up. It was time to get back to business. The task ahead, however, was daunting. The truth is that the representation of athletes is a competitive and economically challenging field. Without emphasizing low fixed costs and high profitability, most new agents fail. There are 300 players drafted, but profitable players are those picked up in the first couple of rounds. Once an agent agrees to represent a client, the next step includes selecting a training facility where they'll prepare for the scouting process. This means the agent assumes the costly responsibility of training the player and providing a per diem for living expenses. In baseball, an agent receives five percent of their athlete's contract, while basketball representatives receive four percent, and in football, agents receive three percent. This makes football representation the highest-risk profession, but it is also the most popular sport in the country, so it draws the most agents.

In 2011, I was approached by a talented Dallas-based marketing executive, Mary McKay, about the upcoming Super Bowl. That year, the game was in Dallas, and she wanted to help me throw one of my iconic Super Bowl parties.

Let's go back down memory lane for a moment. The first Super Bowl party I ever hosted was in 1985 at my house on Panoramic Way in Berkeley. It was a four-story house with redwood and glass, offering a 180-degree view centered on the Golden Gate Bridge across the bay. In attendance were athletes, both current and retired, sports journalists, and some NFL executives, and when I woke up the next morning, there were still some writers sleeping on the couch downstairs. Clearly, we had a good time.

From the beginning, I saw the Super Bowl as more than just a football game. It's a convention of Americana, where big business, big politics, and big entertainment all converge on the host city. I thought, Why not bring everyone together?

But I didn't want to replicate the typical party scene—dark rooms, loud music, and heavy drinking. I wanted something different: a celebration that emphasized community, philanthropy, and meaningful connections. So, I built the parties around raising money for charities like Special Olympics, Make-A-Wish Foundation, and many more. Each year, we also present Humanitarian Awards to recognize the outstanding people behind the sport. Honorees have included team owners like Clark Hunt (Chiefs), Woody Johnson (Jets), Stephen Ross (Dolphins), Mark Davis

(Raiders), and Gayle Benson (Saints), and coaches such as Sean Payton, Andy Reid, and Bruce Arians.

Over the years, we've outgrown living rooms and moved into iconic venues that reflect the spirit of the host city—Jazzland and the New Orleans Jazz Museum, 20th Century Fox Studios and Sony Studios in Los Angeles, and many others. This year, we head to San Francisco for the thirty-ninth edition of the party, and my excitement remains as strong as ever.

I am deeply grateful to continue hosting this tradition. It's one of my favorite times of the year because it brings together such a diverse community. When I was making my business comeback, reviving this event was high on my bucket list. After all, what better way to return than with a Super Bowl party?

Back in 2011, Mary and her team pulled off something truly special. The party was held at Eddy Deen's, a building designed to resemble an indoor dude ranch—straight out of a western movie. We leaned all the way into the Texas theme: I rode a longhorn steer (a sight both ridiculous and unforgettable), we staged armadillo races, and guests enjoyed authentic Texas food stations. The whole venue was transformed into a western spectacle.

Reaching into my network, I invited owners, general managers, players, and members of the press. Even former President George W. Bush had accepted the invitation, though an unexpected ice and snowstorm forced his motorcade to turn back at the last minute.

The place was filled with Dallas Cowboys players, politicians, and famous icons alike, but the night's attention belonged to Texas superstar Earl Campbell. That year at my Super Bowl party, he was a recipient of the Afro-American Hall of Fame award given by founder and civil rights activist Arif Katib, who later inducted me. Earl and I immediately clicked. We began our careers two years apart and, because of that, we had mutual friends and experiences. Earl had flourished in his second career as the owner of a meatpacking company, a rancher, and an entrepreneur. He also had struggled with addiction. I told him about my approach to agenting, and he told me about the dreams he had now that his pro football days were over. He desired to create a health and wellness center in his hometown of Tyler, Texas, and I wanted to help. Over the years, we developed a strong bond and friendship that still thrives today.

It seemed like I was on my way. But in 2012, my financial situation caught up with me, and I had to declare bankruptcy, just when it felt like I was regaining my footing. I had the chance to host the 2012 Super Bowl party, but I thought it best to hold off and demonstrate patience. It did not seem wise to have publicly declared for bankruptcy and have a lavish Super Bowl party in the same year. In that moment, it was vital for me to listen to the environment and the climate that surrounded me. Even though I had no legal obligation to repay creditors, I had a moral obligation. I am committed to repaying all my debts.

Near the end of the year, whispers of my comeback began to spread, and I knew it was time to start a new agency, but I couldn't do it alone. I needed to find a CEO type, someone who could help me get things back up and running. A talented attorney, Adam

Muchnick, was my top choice. After a few of my close friends interviewed him, we came together and decided to create our new firm, Steinberg Sports. I'll never forget the critical role that Adam played in restoring my financial situation. My community and brand came through again when we added marketing executive Amanda Gunville, executive Chris Koras, and a number of interns into the fold. Despite still not being certified as an agent, we began taking small steps toward building our firm. But then, another setback. Our attempts to secure funding failed. One by one, potential investors declined. And without capital, you don't have a firm. Fortunately, my next opportunity arose only a few months later.

In April of 2013, June Jones invited me to come down to SMU and speak to his football squad. I stressed in the speech my role model paradigm and how these football players had a remarkable opportunity to retrace their roots and make a difference off the field. I also emphasized the critical importance of focusing on a career after collegiate or professional sports. I had the unique chance to serve as a mentor to my athletes, and they, too, had the opportunity to give back to their community in a second career. Believe me, if you provide, the world will give back to you in abundance.

June happened to invite an additional man to speak alongside me: David Blanchard. David was a personal coach and proponent of the Og Mandino path to achievement. He also created the Intentional Creation Assessment and Coaching Program. Much of his philosophy is based on Napoleon Hill's teachings in Think and Grow Rich. David was a charismatic, engaging public speaker.

He was accompanied by his friend Scott Irwin. Scott was a successful businessman with an engaging, upbeat outlook on life and a razor-sharp wit. He had grown a niche business (supplying iron pipes for the whole industry) into a wildly successful enterprise.

"What are you looking to do?" Scott asked me that night at dinner. "I'm looking to represent athletes again," I replied, and David and Scott looked at me and said they could put together a group in Houston that would probably be interested in funding me and the new sports agency.

"We believe in you and your mission," they told me. But Scott did more than that. He and his wife, Marylyn, were like guardian angels who supported me until we could make a deal. They put me up in a tiny bedroom, separate from their house, in Houston. That became my base of operations, which I lovingly called my "tree house."

I was blessed enough to have a support system surrounding me. Many friends and acquaintances stepped up and lent me money when I had little. One was my long-term partner, Jeff Moorad, and ironically, another was Dennis

Gilbert, a star MLB agent, who was one of Jeff's biggest rivals in our baseball practice. I explained my circumstances, and he asked how he could help. I did not have the $2,500 to reapply for reinstatement of my NFLPA Agent certification. He drove from his home in Beverly Hills to Newport Beach and handed me a check for the amount. I also received support calls from a variety of people. One I really enjoyed was from NBA star and commentator Charles Barkley.

Scott invited me to Houston to pitch my agency funding proposal to a group of investors. The most significant potential partners were Gale and Trisha Oliver. Gale, a successful businessman in oil and gas and an ex-Texas A&M football player, could launch us on his own. I was excited to present, so I invited my good friend Earl Campbell to come along.

Earl is an icon in Texas and cannot walk a street without being mobbed. With Earl by my side, I gave my best presentation on how I envisioned the future of Steinberg Sports. I wanted to build a sports agency like the world had never seen before. As with my old agencies, the primary focus would be on finding unique athletes who would fit into role-model positions. But I also wanted to expand into other fields such as entertainment and media. I explained to the potential investors that sports and entertainment were merging. The new agency could create entertainment programming for television, motion pictures, and the internet. I envisioned an agency that could provide a steady supply of content for reality shows, documentaries, dramatically scripted motion pictures and television, video games, podcasts, radio shows, and books.

Soon after the meeting, Scott, Gale Oliver, Julie Stagner, Bill Dore, and Andy Priest signed on as early investors. Cosmo De Nicola, a talented serial entrepreneur, later joined. Soon after, he and I launched philanthropic awards highlighting the charitable and community programs that NFL owners, general managers, coaches, players, and retired players created for their achievements. The original plan was to open an office in Newport Beach and then a branch in Houston, slowly building out throughout Texas. The state is a golden goose for producing young athletes. The hub of universities in Texas provides a vibrant talent pipeline that would help rebuild my practice.

Adding the Texas pipeline to our primary West Coast base would significantly increase the number of prospects. We cultivated a vast network of coaches, scouts, trainers, family members, pastors, and local attorneys, among others. Too many agents focus solely on the player, failing to recognize that the athlete listens to advice from multiple mentors and influencers.

Before my crash, I'd given over 3,000 speeches and established a massive infrastructure, but I worried that being away from active representation for six years might have eroded it. But it happened that a marketing executive friend of mine was conducting consumer research for people exiting the Delta Center, home of the Utah Jazz. He threw in a question for my benefit, asking people if they could name a sports agent, and fifty-one percent named me, forty percent said "Jerry Maguire," and the rest were divided between Scott Boras and Drew Rosenhaus. That was a revelation.

Although I was still remembered, between the time I gave up my practice in 2007 and my return in 2013, a whole new generation of athletes had emerged. Their primary sources of information were the internet and their cell phones. They were technologically advanced and had grown up in an era of athletic branding. Their tolerance for long, drawn-out meetings and presentations was much shorter. I needed to find creative ways to introduce myself to that generation. To build this new agency, I needed to rethink my approach. I needed to prioritize the first steps first, in order of their importance. My first job was to pass the test that the NFLPA required to become certified as an agent. I had mastered the salary cap rules starting in 1993, but I had some catching up to do.

I coined the term "caponomics" in an interview with Gordon Forbes of USA Today in the early days of the cap. As a firm, we had creatively introduced a series of clever contract structures that allowed players and teams to construct robust compensation contracts while minimizing the cap consequences. But the 2010 collective bargaining agreement introduced a brave new world of salary-cap definitions and lexicon. With the new rules, it was like trying to learn Chinese after a lifetime of speaking English. But I passed the NFLPA test. With the test behind me, I next focused on expanding recognition and brand. Back in 2010, while in sober living, I had massive amounts of free time. I felt that writing a book and taking a press tour were good ways to reintroduce myself. I contacted a potential co-writer, Allen Abrahamson, and began retracing my life for my memoir. So, I spent hours talking about my life and career with Allen, but he had to abandon the project because of family emergencies, unfortunately. I was lucky to find another talented co-author, Michael Arkush, who continued the process. I found the exercise to be therapeutic. I had spent virtually no time being introspective in the previous years.

One achievement led to another. My book The Agent, which I had worked on while at sober living, was finally published in January of 2014. It quickly became a New York Times bestseller.

To bring exposure to the book, publishers like to get authors on a road trip across the country. My book tour started in New York City the week before my 2014 Super Bowl Party.

That year, I flew back to New York. A unique and catastrophic weather pattern nicknamed the "Arctic Vortex" had just descended on the city. The temperatures were as low as four degrees, the streets were icy, and a bitter wind hurled snow everywhere. We had a whole series of interviews scheduled, and I felt like a popsicle. Having grown up in Southern California, my cold tolerance was very low, and I had no idea how to keep my balance on the icy streets. It was hard to function with tons of snow blowing right in my face. Somehow, I managed to cross all over Manhattan as I appeared on The Today Show, CNN, CNBC, Fox and Friends, Newsmax, MSNBC, and many other media outlets to talk about my book. That week was the start of numerous interviews in print, on the radio, and on television.

Then it was time for my first Super Bowl party with our new firm. It was held in Manhattan on top of a skyscraper with a 360-degree view of the city. We pulled out all the stops for this one. Guests sauntered down a red carpet, as microphone-toting journalists peppered them with questions and flashbulbs popped. Celebrities like actor Kevin Costner, singer Wynonna Judd, and Dancing with the Stars performer Karina Smirnoff were in attendance. We invited cadets from West Point and first responders to recognize their sacrifice and hard work. A live television hookup was set up with Fox's Brian Kilmeade and connected to a group of soldiers in Iraq so they could participate and talk to the celebrities.

Quarterback Steve Young gave an especially inspirational talk to the soldiers. We raised money for charity with a silent auction. I signed dozens of copies of my new book.

I peered across a crowded party filled with joy and laughter and had this thought: I guess I am sorta back.

It seemed like a dream.

Chapter 9

Adaptability: Jukes and Cuts

Willie Bioff was a very famous bank robber and was asked why he robbed banks. His response was because that's where the money is. Now, I had to think like Willie Bioff. I had to think where the potential new clients were—on college campuses. And to find them, I needed to be resourceful. There is an abundance of talented young athletes on college campuses, so there I went. The key here was introducing myself to the new generation, who might not have been familiar with me because of my six years out of the business. To these young athletes, six years felt like an eternity.

We didn't have the funds to compete with some of the top agencies; even before my crash, ours was a boutique firm that relied on our ability to connect with players rather than entice them with inflated upfront payments. Plus, the game had changed in just a few years. And I wasn't the same man, either. So, if I were going to replicate my success, it wouldn't be with the same playbook. And that required another skill: being innovative.

In your own comeback, whatever form it takes, you will likely find yourself in the same position: having to rebuild with fewer resources, bigger challenges, and a different world than you are used to. You must find ways to adapt to the circumstances. My book tour continued after the Super Bowl. In 2014, I traveled to almost fifty campuses, giving speeches about the current status and opportunities in the world of sports business as I crisscrossed the country from the University of Washington to the University of Miami. At the University of Michigan, I reunited with my old client, now-Head Coach Jim Harbaugh. I always found Jim to be warm and funny, a contrast with his stern demeanor seen on the sidelines. And he was interesting and well-rounded with eclectic interests. He has a unique ability to motivate.

I spoke to undergrads, to sports marketing majors, and at business and law schools. While I was on those campuses, I met with head and assistant coaches, athletic directors, and support personnel. This helped me reestablish an infrastructure. It also helped me understand the new landscape of college athletics, their athletes, and the people who wanted to have a future career in the business of sports.

I remember meeting Greg Byrne, the Athletic Director at the University of Arizona, who is currently the Athletic Director at the University of Alabama. He had vision and creativity. Greg had created a unique program based on the life skills a student-athlete would need later in life. He knew that only a tiny percentage of college athletes will ever make it to the pros. So, hundreds of thousands of athletes give their all for their university, but upon graduation, will face the challenges of adjusting to a non-athletic career. He had a comprehensive booklet that taught athletes about topics ranging from proper etiquette to financial literacy to second-career preparation. This education prepared every college athlete for the challenges they would later face.

In Texas, I did a mega tour of TCU, where my talented former associate Jeremiah Donati was soon to become Athletic Director at SMU, Baylor, Rice, the University of Texas, the University of Houston, and Texas A&M. The facilities at Texas A&M were stunning. Their women's track stadium—and every other building—was state-of-the-art. And the students were the most courteous and kind that I had ever met.

The most stunning athletic facility I experienced was at the University of Oregon. They had top-tier equipment and facilities that were more comprehensive than many professional teams. Phil Knight and Nike were the driving force behind much of the funding. The sight of the crowd that came to hear my talk was mind-boggling. Their enthusiasm was palpable. I also spoke at the University of Ohio and the University of San Francisco, both of which have strong sports management programs.

Sports and media go hand in hand and, in the athletic community, new platforms have replaced the TV, radio, and newspapers that dominated in my youth. I still read four newspapers a day, several magazines a week, and believe that the depth of reporting allows me to have a clearer vision of where business and society are heading. But athletes and fans were spending endless hours on their cell phones and computers. I had to familiarize myself with social media and became acquainted with Instagram, Twitter (to a lesser extent), LinkedIn, and Facebook, and later TikTok. I expanded my reach by posting on social media. I began posting opinions, pictures, and stories about athletes on all these forums. I created a one-minute segment of advice called Wednesday Wisdom.

For #WednesdayWisdom, I share different pieces of advice I have learned over my lifetime. Things like, be careful not to say the most hurtful things on your mind because those insults will never be forgotten. Or your goal in driving is to get from here to there safely, not to engage in confrontations with other drivers that you have never met and will never see again (that one works on both a literal and metaphorical level). I also quoted a plaque my father had in his office that read: Of all our problems, great and small, the greatest are those that never happen at all.

My topics vary from personal advice and health and wellness to the importance of networking. I needed to establish myself as someone who was dependable, knowledgeable, and tech-savvy. All of this was essential to returning to agenting, as was calculating the impact of high school and college athletes being able to hire a marketing director and receive money for endorsements, as well as it being a tool in college recruiting. The thought of making a pitch to a fifteen-year-old who may not be mature enough to appreciate our role modeling and second-career emphasis was not very appealing to me. And not to mention all the changes that have happened and are still happening in the field. If Rip Van Winkle had begun his slumber in 1975, the year I entered the profession, and awoke in 2025, he would hardly recognize the sports industry. The landscape has been reshaped beyond recognition. For anyone entering the field today, three earth-shattering developments have fundamentally altered college sports, the agent business, and the culture of athletics itself.

The first and most transformative change is the rise of NIL—the right for athletes to profit from their name, image, and likeness. This concept, once unimaginable, now defines the recruiting landscape and the careers of young athletes. Athletes as young as fifteen are branding themselves, hiring marketing directors, and negotiating endorsement deals. NIL has turned high school and college recruiting into the equivalent of NFL free agency, with bidding wars replacing traditional recruiting pitches.

One striking example came when a quarterback originally committed to LSU, only to flip when Michigan's collective reportedly offered him $14 million to decommit and join their program. Wealthy alumni bases now dictate recruiting power, creating an uneven playing field and widening the gap between the top four athletic conferences and the rest of the country. These powerhouse conferences, backed by wealthy donors, now operate like the major leagues, while the other programs risk becoming minor-league feeder teams. The dynamic mirrors income inequality in the broader economy, where a few elite programs consolidate power and resources while others are left behind.

The sums of money involved are staggering. In 2024, Duke basketball phenom Cooper Flagg became the single biggest beneficiary of NIL, earning an estimated twenty-eight million dollars in a single year. To put this in perspective, when Flagg enters the NBA as the unanimous first overall pick, his rookie contract will pay him roughly twelve-and-a-half million dollars annually, meaning he will actually take a fifty percent pay cut moving from college to the professional ranks. What once was the apex of financial opportunity has shifted.

For elite prospects, the road to wealth and stardom now begins in high school or college, long before their first professional game. Other examples confirm the scope of this change. USC quarterback Caleb Williams made millions of dollars as a college player through deals with Dr. Pepper, Wendy's, and other national brands. For decades, I advocated for better compensation for college athletes, particularly given the billions generated through television contracts, ticket sales, and merchandise. Yet the rollout of NIL resembled the Oklahoma land rush: chaotic, uneven, and poorly regulated. Collectives quickly formed to pool endorsement money for recruits, and the transfer portal became a second front in the same bidding wars. The old ideals of recruiting grounded student-athletes with strong families and long-term career thinking have given way to short-term financial compensation. Fifteen-year-olds and their parents now negotiate like free agents, often with little interest in role modeling or post-career planning.

The concept of amateurism had always been strained, with under-the-table payments, gifts, and favors circulating in violation of NCAA rules. NIL has simply made official what was often happening unofficially, but it has also exposed new problems. One is the inequality within teams themselves. How does an anonymous offensive lineman feel when his quarterback earns millions through NIL while he earns nothing, despite the fact that the quarterback cannot succeed without his protection? Football is the ultimate team game, yet NIL rewards a handful of stars while ignoring the majority. That tension could fracture locker rooms and undercut the spirit of team play.

The second major transformation is the breakup of traditional conferences and widespread realignment. The Pac-12's collapse illustrates the upheaval. Cal and Stanford, once fixtures on the Pacific Coast, now compete in the Atlantic Coast Conference, whose name reflects geography on the opposite side of the country. Rivalries that defined college sports are disappearing. USC versus Stanford or UCLA versus Cal, once annual traditions, have been sacrificed for the pursuit of television revenue.

The driving force behind realignment is access to larger media markets. The Big Ten now stretches from New Jersey to California, ensuring coverage in the number one New York market, the number two Los Angeles market, and the number three Chicago market. Academic integrity suffers when student-athletes are required to travel across the country for conference games. A six-hour flight to New Jersey, combined with the demands of training and competition, makes it nearly impossible to balance coursework and athletics. The long-term implication is that four or five super-conferences, enriched by elevated television contracts and wealthy alumni bases, will pull away from the rest of the NCAA. Once these super-conferences realize they no longer need the NCAA as a middleman, they will likely negotiate their own broadcast contracts and establish their own rules. That will leave smaller programs behind, creating a tiered system of haves and have-nots.

Because football and basketball drive revenue, other sports such as gymnastics, wrestling, and swimming will be marginalized or eliminated. This undermines the educational mission of providing athletic opportunities to the largest number of students. Furthermore, the reshuffling will inevitably raise questions of Title IX compliance, as universities attempt to balance men's and women's programs while chasing football and basketball revenue.

A related development that further upended the foundation of college sports came with the House v. NCAA decision in 2024. In that landmark antitrust case, the courts ruled that the NCAA had unlawfully suppressed athlete compensation for decades. The settlement requires the NCAA and its member schools to pay nearly three billion dollars in damages to former college athletes who were denied the opportunity to profit from their names, images, and likenesses. Just as important, the ruling effectively ended the notion that the NCAA could set strict limits on athlete pay going forward. Schools will now be allowed to share a portion of their athletic department revenue directly with players, ushering in a quasi-professional model within college sports.

The ripple effects are enormous. Universities must now budget for athlete payrolls, which will inevitably concentrate resources even further into the hands of schools with the wealthiest boosters and deepest television contracts. Title IX compliance becomes even more complex when revenue-sharing is introduced, forcing institutions to weigh gender equity obligations against the financial demands of football and men's basketball. For decades, the NCAA leaned on the ideal of amateurism as both a shield and a justification, but House stripped away that façade. What was once presented as education-first competition has been legally redefined as a commercial enterprise, and that acknowledgment changes the way fans, athletes, and administrators view the entire system. The third profound change is the integration of legalized gambling into professional and collegiate sports. For decades, gambling was considered an existential threat to the integrity of competition. There was a clear and unbreachable wall separating sports from betting. That wall has now crumbled. Following a court decision in New Jersey that overturned federal restrictions, thirty-two states now allow legalized sports gambling. Sportsbooks operate inside or adjacent to major stadiums, including Northwest Stadium in Washington, Wrigley Field in Chicago, and Progressive Field in Cleveland. Fans can buy a hot dog and place a wager in the same transaction.

Television broadcasts and social media feeds are saturated with advertising for FanDuel, DraftKings, and other betting platforms. The sheer volume of promotion ensures that gambling is unavoidable for anyone watching a game. This normalization carries dangers. A certain percentage of fans will inevitably become addicted, risking financial ruin. More importantly, the relationship between athletes and gambling creates opportunities for corruption that could erode public trust in fair competition.

Recent cases illustrate the risk. NBA forward Jontay Porter reportedly shared inside information with gamblers, revealing that he planned to exit games early. This enabled bettors to exploit new prop bets, which allow wagers on individual performance within a game, such as total points scored or minutes played. Using inside information, gamblers profited handsomely while the integrity of the contest was compromised. Similarly, in Major League Baseball, Shohei Ohtani's interpreter misused his access to Ohtani's accounts, diverting eighteen million dollars to cover gambling debts. While Ohtani himself was cleared of wrongdoing, the scandal demonstrates how quickly reputations can be put at risk.

The greatest threat to sports is not dwindling attendance or declining ratings. Fans will always flock to arenas and tune in to watch games. Revenues from television contracts, merchandising, and stadium deals continue to rise. The true existential threat is the perception that games are not contested honestly. If fans believe that outcomes are fixed or manipulated by gambling interests, the legitimacy of the entire enterprise collapses. Wrestling thrives as entertainment because no one mistakes it for a true athletic contest. Sports are different. Their very essence depends on the belief that the competition is genuine. Taken together, NIL, conference realignment, and legalized gambling have permanently altered the sports industry. Opportunities for athletes to profit have expanded dramatically, television revenues have reached new heights, and fan engagement remains strong. Yet the risks are equally significant. Inequality among athletes and programs has widened, traditional rivalries have been sacrificed for financial gain, and the integrity of competition is more vulnerable than ever.

For those of us who have lived through five decades in this business, the transformation is staggering. For those entering today, it is simply the new normal—the brave new world of 2025 bears little resemblance to the landscape of 1975. The industry is larger, wealthier, and more complex, but also more precarious. The challenge for the next generation will be to protect the spirit of competition and the values that made sports such a vital part of American life in the first place, even as the pressures of money, media, and gambling reshape it before our eyes. In the midst of that shifting terrain, I found myself rediscovering parts of who I was before the chaos—returning to the creative instincts that had always driven me, long before contracts and clients defined my days. I also tapped into long-abandoned passions, like writing, which served me well. When I was nine, I published my own newspaper and, since we lived on Corinth Drive, it was called The Corinthian; its banner read "The Corinthian Upholds the Truth." I wrote for every student newspaper. Later in life, I dabbled in writing sporadically, but I have rediscovered my enjoyment of it. It wasn't just a passion project; it was vital to getting my name out there. I wrote columns for Forbes, opinion pieces for newspapers like the New York Times and Los Angeles Times, book reviews, movie reviews, and magazine articles.

I enjoyed meeting other people and public speaking, so I spoke to business groups, legal groups, charitable fundraisers, and academia. Sometimes I philosophized about values and shared stories about my father's shining example; other times I lectured about the business of sports: TV revenue, building new stadiums, the art of negotiation, how to listen and do business with empathy. I also spoke about my experience as a technical advisor for sports-themed motion pictures: Jerry Maguire, Any Given Sunday, and For the Love of the Game.

I shared the story of how writer-director Cameron Crowe shadowed me for a couple of years, following me everywhere: the NFL Draft, league meetings, games, my Super Bowl party, even Pro Scouting Day. Along the way, I told him countless stories about my life and experiences.

As technical advisor on Jerry Maguire, part of my role was to vet the script so that true sports fans would recognize the settings and dialogue as authentic. One of the more memorable moments was taking Cuba Gooding Jr., who played wide receiver Rod Tidwell, to the Super Bowl in Arizona. I introduced him in character as one of my clients, and he spent the week alongside wide receivers Desmond Howard and Amani Toomer.

When the film was released, Jerry Maguire became the highest-grossing sports movie in history. To this day, I can hardly walk through an airport or sit down to dinner without someone running up and shouting the four words that became iconic: "Show me the money!" That moment in popular culture inspired me to use my own platform far beyond sports. I wanted to use that visibility for something impactful. I like teaching and mentoring, so the interactions on those college campuses were significant to me.

After all, teaching and mentoring were in my blood, and I was proud to carry on my father's legacy as an educator. I allocated roughly one third of my time to working on charities and projects that made a positive difference in the world. The University of California, Irvine created a new law school with visionary dean Erwin Chemerinsky. He implemented a policy that gave every first-year student a full scholarship, enabling them to attract some of the best students in the country immediately.

I taught a semester of Sports Law there. I also taught a semester at Chapman University Law School and a semester of Sports Business at Concordia University Irvine. But the reality is that there really isn't much compelling information that constitutes sports law. It is the law affecting heavily compensated individuals. The players' associations and management negotiate the collective bargaining agreements, so an individual practitioner cannot change the terms or language. There are also standard player contracts—boilerplate—and standard representation agreements. So, it made more sense to me to do a class focused on interactivity, with students doing exercises on recruiting, negotiating, branding and marketing, and setting up a charitable foundation. I took one group to an Angels game and had them focus on branding and marketing opportunities. I had Jacob Ullman, Senior Vice President of Production and Talent Development at FOX, come and instruct the students on how to obtain a position at his network.

I also had Robert Hacker, Vice President of Business and Legal Affairs at FOX Sports, come to the class and negotiate an on-air talent contract with the students.

We gave them a damage-control problem: they had to hold a press conference to defend troubled athletes. Combining all these fields made me think about what I did every day—not as my life's work, but as activities I would have chosen to do anyway. Doing what you love ignites a passion and motivation that makes the endless hours meaningful.

This was an unusual path back to sports agenting. But engineering a comeback doesn't mean retreading the same ground you've walked on before. You blaze a new trail by being flexible. Think on your feet, approach the task at hand with an innovative, open mind, and the way will open up before you.

THE ROAD TO AGENCY

Gale and Garrett Gilbert

As I said before, if I was going to rebuild the company, I would have to do a lot with a little. Making a comeback forces you to be scrappy, innovative, and tenacious. My competitors had deeper human resources, larger bank accounts, and reputations unsullied by scandal. But I still had the things that had always given me a competitive advantage, advantages you can't really put a price on or quantify: a keen understanding of what players need and want and a duty-bound dedication to advocating for them.

Earlier in my career, I represented a client named Gale Gilbert, who was a quarterback at my alma mater, the University of California at Berkeley. The Cal football clients I had over the years (forty in total) were always special to me because we attended the same alma mater. Gale was an excellent passer and had an engaging personality. As a pro, he went on to play for the Seattle Seahawks. He became the only player in NFL history to play in five consecutive Super Bowls, four with the Buffalo Bills and one with the San Diego Chargers. In retirement, he moved his family to Austin, Texas, and, to no surprise, his son Garrett followed in his footsteps with his athletic abilities and friendly, warm demeanor. That year, in the draft, Derrick Carr was a talented quarterback, and he was projected to be selected early in the first round. But then he began slipping and sliding into the second round, into Garrett's territory. It's in our interest to have every quarterback projected to be a first-round pick selected, so the Raiders would then have a clear path to Garrett. But now that Derrick was still in play, I started to feel anxious about the possibility that the Raiders might draft Carr.

When the Raiders' turn came up, they selected Derrick Carr. In that moment in Gilbert's house, it was as if a balloon had been pierced by a pin, releasing all the optimism as we quietly accepted this unfortunate plot twist. The only other team with an intense interest in taking Garrett was the St. Louis Rams.

In the second round, he wasn't selected. In the third round, he wasn't selected.

Finally, he was picked in the sixth round. All the disappointment of the previous days was forgotten. Garrett's ability to persevere in the face of doubts led to this moment. The mood in the room completely changed. It erupted in celebration. Support calls started pouring in, and Garrett spoke with his new coach, who discussed everything a rookie needs to know. The sixth round wasn't what Garrett had hoped for, but to put it in perspective, there were thousands of young men hoping to hear their name called on draft day, and Garrett was one of the 300 chosen ones. He would still have a chance to make an impact. Steinberg Sports was back; we had a draft pick!

Garrett Gilbert's signing with the Rams gave me a wave of renewed energy to keep my comeback going. In searching for ways to redefine what it meant to be a sports agent, I also wanted to redefine the meaning of quarterbacks or create a new type of quarterback that stood above the rest. I've always realized how valuable quarterback clients could be.

PAXTON LYNCH

As the agency continued to develop, I added a young attorney, Chris Cabott, from Philadelphia. He had the energy necessary to help rebuild. We added my brilliant middle son, Matt Steinberg, who was a certified agent. We also added Selwyn Roberts, an agent with social media and marketing skills. Together, we brainstormed how to build out our client roster.

A young quarterback named Paxton Lynch fit the definition of a franchise quarterback perfectly. In 2015, I received a call from a man named David Lynch. At first, I thought it was the David Lynch who directed Twin Peaks and Eraserhead, but it was even better. David was a father who believed that his son was born to play in the NFL, and he was right. When I discovered Paxton, he was on the brink of his own comeback story. He was relatively new to football yet clearly had the talent to thrive. Standing 6'6", he was a handsome young man with a bubbly personality. I could see that he would do well as a role model for the younger generation. His family was just as impressive as he. The Lynch family was a close-knit unit that rooted itself in

Christianity, and Paxton's mom, Stacie, was the epitome of a loving mother.

Before I stepped into the Lynch house, I had to be brutally honest with myself and face the hard questions. I knew I had no divine right to represent any athlete; each player and family had their own needs and were searching for the right person to meet them. They deserved the freedom to ask any questions about my background and practice—and the only proper response was complete transparency.

I was sixty-seven years old—would I be able to support their son for his entire career? Here I was hoping my 15,000 steps a day and working out three times a week would work in my favor and spare me a few years.

How could I promise I'd stay sober? The truth was, I couldn't promise future sobriety; there is no ethical way to make such a claim. The best I could do was describe my activities and commitment to maintaining sobriety. Many of the families I was talking to were familiar with the consequences of alcohol abuse. Not all responded favorably. I remember one parent hanging up the phone as soon as I introduced myself. "I don't believe alcoholics can ever be cured," he said. Fortunately, my clients' parents were forgiving and cared much more about the future than the past. My clients seemed to appreciate my honesty about life and business and leaned on me for guidance.

After holding the initial meeting with the Lynch family, it was finally time to present to Paxton himself. I've met with players in fancy restaurants, college dorms, and family living rooms, but to pitch Paxton, I went to a house that he shared with four roommates, with whom he seemed to be best friends. They were hilarious together. Their home was truly a college bachelor pad, a la Animal House, replete with cups they recycled from the nearby 7-Elevens.

As I was pitching Paxton, I sat on a couch that was so old that I literally kept sliding off it onto the floor! Despite the slippery couch, the visit went well, and Paxton agreed to sign with Steinberg Sports. We were excited to have the opportunity to begin his path to the draft. Paxton planned to declare for the draft at the end of his junior year, forgoing his last year of eligibility. Many players declare at the end of their junior year, but I wanted Paxton to stand out above the rest. This was a significant decision that deserved a major announcement.

As Paxton was making his exit from college, we didn't want it to seem like a rushed process but rather a carefully calculated decision. The best setting was for Paxton to sit at his press conference with his mother, father, and the coach, presenting a united front as he announced he was leaving. The second thing I knew we needed to do was keep him bonded to his university and alumni, so we could start gathering their support. Therefore, at the press conference, he proudly stated, "I'll be a Memphis Tiger for life!"

While Paxton stayed in Orlando to train with famous quarterback coach David Morris for the Combine and Pro Scouting Day, I began brainstorming with my team about his brand. What was a catchphrase, or a graphic image, that perfectly summed him up? In the middle of the discussions, just like that, it dawned on me: "Faith, Family, Football ... Paxton Lynch." It summed him up to a tee, giving him an elevator pitch when it was time to start networking. Paxton took a break from training and came to San Francisco for the Super Bowl festivities. We wanted to raise his profile, and every year at the Super Bowl, they have something called Radio Row. It's a couple hundred talk radio shows and some

TV channels all under one roof. At Radio Row, I do fifty to seventy interviews over the span of forty-eight hours. Talk about going hoarse. Reporters and I discuss topics such as the quarterback matchup in the game, who I think will win, our annual Super Bowl party, leading industry trends, and endorsement possibilities from the Super Bowl.

What I was attempting to do was brand Paxton Lynch as a franchise quarterback. In every interview, when I was asked about

Paxton, I led with Faith, Family, Football—Paxton Lynch and Franchise Quarterback. This approach didn't replace scouting, but the goal was to plant the seed in the minds of the public, as well as scouts, owners, and coaches.

On Radio Row, Paxton conducted interviews with outlets in Miami, Washington, New York, Buffalo, Cincinnati, and more. With each interview, we were raising his profile and expanding his reach. Another benefit of Radio Row is that owners, general managers, and coaches are also dropping by to be interviewed, and this became an opportunity for Paxton to start meeting people. During the NFL draft, top-rated players have the chance to fly into whatever location the draft is being held at that year. Some players travel to the city where the NFL draft is held, while others choose a local venue. There are limitations on how many extended family members and friends can share the day with the player on-site. Paxton wanted to be surrounded by his family and friends, so rather than flying into Chicago, I traveled to Deltona, Florida. Paxton chose a bowling alley as the site for his draft day party. Fun, right? Paxton wanted a respite from the super tension that comes with waiting endlessly to be picked, so he and his friends were temporarily distracted by bowling.

Each team in the first round has ten minutes to make its selection. While other players were agonizing over watching the draft, Paxton passed the time throwing strikes at the bowling alley. As the draft proceeded and reached around the twentieth pick in the first round, Paxton adjourned to the parking lot, where he and his friends played catch with a football. At the twenty-sixth pick, it was announced that Denver had made a trade. Denver team president John Elway called my cell. He wanted to talk to Paxton to tell him that the Broncos had selected him as the twenty-sixth pick in the first round of the 2016 NFL draft. Paxton's first-round draft pick marked the return to what had been my hallmark: first-round quarterbacks. We yelled out into the parking lot to bring Paxton to the phone and, all of a sudden, pandemonium broke loose. Friends and family were hugging, shouting, and crying, and the mood was euphoric. Paxton was heading to the NFL.

PATRICK MAHOMES

In 2016, I traveled to a town in East Texas—Tyler—which was known for producing talented athletes. One of those athletes was Houston Oilers Hall of Fame running back Earl Campbell. My former client, ex-Ravens cornerback Gary Baxter, and Earl were attempting to establish a unique health and wellness treatment center in their hometown. Earl and I had become close friends, and I wanted to help support this effort. One night, the mayor of Tyler and his wife joined us for dinner. The mayor's wife was a big Texas Tech fan and couldn't stop talking about a young, gifted athlete from Tyler named Patrick Mahomes.

"But don't worry about him, he's going to play professional baseball," she said as if she had inside information, but she only managed to ignite my interest.

Despite the mayor's wife's warning, my team decided to do our research. We got our hands on some film footage and were blown away. We saw the undeniable truth: this athlete had otherworldly tools and an unbelievable arm. We set a meeting with his parents, Randi and Patrick Sr., in a restaurant in Grapevine, Texas. His parents were playing the role of protective agents, screening him. In most cases, we would meet with parents or other family members who adopted a series of questions to help them do fiduciary screening of the hundreds of agents approaching them.

Big Pat (Patrick's dad) was tall and engaging; the attention was drawn to him in any room he entered. Pat had a long career as a baseball relief pitcher, and young Patrick had grown up in that environment. Patrick's mom, Randi, was beautiful with a movie-star presence and a vivid sense of humor. She was a loving and concerned mother. Mia, Patrick's half-sister, was there for the meeting, as well. You could see she would one day be a talented athlete, given the way she was throwing a toy football in our meeting. I was ready to present our best case for signing with us, but the only issue was the restaurant.

Loud music and poor acoustics made the environment challenging for anyone to present, but it was an extra barrier for me. I do not have a naturally loud voice. I couldn't hear clearly, and within the first five minutes it was tough to distinguish what the person right in front of me was saying from the background noise. The fatal blend of background noise and table chatter translated into a Tower of Babel. Unless the Mahomes family came equipped with closed captioning, I was in trouble. But this challenging environment was not new to me. As an agent, you have to be able to adapt to whatever the situation or environment might be.

So, it was time to begin. I knew my presentation was solid because of the number of first-round draft picks, first overall picks, and Hall of Fame players who were my clients. It is critical to put oneself into the heart and mind of the parents and not make assumptions about what they are looking for. The key to a long, successful relationship is serving a client's needs. So, I asked the Mahomes a series of questions to draw out their priorities. I wanted them to know more than just my accomplishments, but to be comfortable with our holistic approach. To notice that I wasn't just a regular agent. I wanted them to know that helping their son get into the NFL was just the first part of the journey. I tried to set the stage where Patrick could use his platform for good beyond the football field. I talked to the family about role modeling and helping Patrick to retrace his roots. Revisiting his high school and college communities and setting up a charitable foundation in his professional city, which would help establish the genesis of his second career. I had been able to watch a series of interviews featuring Patrick, in which he was very articulate and had a good sense of humor. He could be a superb role model to his community in Tyler, Lubbock, and his hometown.

This approach would lay the groundwork for Patrick to not only be a football star but to leave a legacy. We had the opportunity to talk about the path to the draft, the ins and outs of contracts, and the salary cap. We also discussed the different branding and marketing opportunities that could position Patrick as an entrepreneur. I also emphasized the importance of long-term health, especially when it comes to concussions, a topic that agents too often avoid. "Look," I told the Mahomes family, "most athletes are going to be in denial about the impact of a concussion if, and when, they have the misfortune of suffering one. That's why it's critical that you, as his family, pledge now: if a serious injury occurs, you'll advocate for his long-term health above all else. When it comes to decisions about getting back in the game after a concussion, our top priority must be ensuring he can live a long, healthy, and productive life after football."

Ensuring the long-term well-being of the athletes I represent has always been close to my heart, and I will further discuss this later in the book. I emphasized that the key to Patrick's future success was the nature of the franchise that drafted him. Stability at the ownership level, excellence at the front office, and a gifted coach with a plan were critical. He needed a franchise that knew how to develop a young quarterback but also offered a strong supporting cast. In the long run, it was not as important how high he was drafted but that he could end up with a franchise that would give him the best chance for a long and productive career.

Excitedly, they were interested in everything we had to offer; they wanted an agent who would enhance their son. Someone who would help shape his football career in the years to come, while also finding a way to utilize his platform to help others.

We went on to attend a couple of Patrick's college games. One happened to be on his birthday, which allowed us to have a celebratory dinner afterwards. During this time, we strengthened our bond and relationship with Patrick and his family. We were slowly earning their trust. Trust is key in the agentry business. I was sincere, and I wanted them to believe in us enough to take their son into the draft because, despite early projections, we recognized Patrick's greatness from a mile away.

Many franchises stereotyped Patrick as a gunslinger—a player with a strong arm but not enough discipline. They pointed out that, in coach Kliff Kingsbury's system, he would receive the snap in the backfield instead of taking the ball under center. It was clear why they were miscategorizing him, but they were not correctly projecting him into the future. In the pro game, the quarterback takes the snap under center, but in college, he takes the snap from the backfield. Patrick also played on a team with a weak defense, which often led them to give up fifty points a game. This meant he was pressured to score a touchdown on every drive and try to win every game with his arm.

The key to Patrick's scouting was the ability to show scouts that he could function under center with a three, five, seven-step drop. We recognized a franchise quarterback when we saw one. Even though some teams projected him as low as a third-round pick, we thought he should go high in the first round.

In January, Patrick signed up for a comprehensive pre-scouting program. He chose to train at Exos, a training facility in Carlsbad, California, some thirty miles north of San Diego. He was coached by a quarterback guru named Dave Shepherd, who further honed his talents. Later that month, we flew Patrick to Houston for Super Bowl 2017. Like Paxton, we brought him to Radio Row where he shined. He wore a suit, was handsome, and he charmed everyone with his warm personality and fantastic sense of humor. I sat back and watched in awe as he made friends and left a lasting impression everywhere he went. He also met the general managers, owners, and coaches who circulated on Radio Row. They needed to see that he was a franchise quarterback with an eidetic memory and a gifted arm. Early on in the path to the draft, Patrick caught the eye of Clark Hunt, the owner of the Kansas Chiefs, as well as John Dorsey, the General

Manager, and Brett Veach, the Assistant General Manager. Chris had a close relationship with Brett Veach, and Clark and I had a long-term relationship. I had been close friends with Clark's father, owner Lamar Hunt, since the seventies. In fact, the first time I met Clark and his brother Danny was when they were ball boys with the Chiefs.

I'd known them for their whole lives. I'd also represented major Chiefs stars before, including Hall of Fame linebacker Derrick Thomas, safety Deron Cherry, placekicker Nick Lowery, and Hall of Fame tight end Tony Gonzalez. I had discussions with Clark over the years on the quarterback question and why it was important to have a franchise quarterback leading his team.

At the Scouting Combine in Indianapolis, Patrick exhibited excellent throwing skills. But the real test would come at Pro Scouting Day, the centerpiece of quarterback scouting, held at the players' university stadium. Dozens of scouts assembled at Texas Tech in Lubbock, Texas, where Patrick put on a stunning throwing clinic. He completed virtually every pass. He took the ball under center and performed the three, five, seven drop flawlessly. It truly was a thing of beauty.

At the grand finale, he threw a pass standing at the twenty-five-yard line, across the fifty, and all the way into the other end zone. There were oohs and awws from the scouts, and news of his spectacular afternoon zipped around the league, creating instant interest and elevation in his draft status. It was now time for the draft. Patrick decided to stay in Tyler and invite everyone important to him to share in the celebration. Kansas City had the twenty-sixth pick in the first round, but teams like New Orleans and Houston liked Patrick and were ahead of Kansas City in the draft order. The Chiefs executed a perfect trade and moved up into the tenth slot and drafted Patrick. The country club erupted into absolute chaos.

In 2016, we had the twenty-sixth player in the first round as a client, and now, in 2017, we had the tenth pick in the first round. I was traveling down the road of my comeback. It was a positive that the Chiefs already had Alex Smith playing as the starting quarterback. Patrick was anxious to play, like any competitive player. But the adjustment to the speed and complexity of pro football is a major learning curve. When a rookie quarterback makes rookie mistakes, he can lose the trust of the organization and the fans. With Alex Smith at the helm, Patrick could sit back, watch, and learn in his rookie season. Alex Smith was a generous mentor. The critical issue wasn't how quickly Patrick could start, but that he would be well-prepared when that chance came.

In 2018, Patrick had one of the most electrifying debut seasons in the history of the NFL. He threw sixteen touchdown passes in his first four games. He exhibited a unique, unprecedented style, featuring no-look passes, throwing with his left arm, escaping pressure in the pocket, and extending plays for extended periods, enabling him to throw to wide receiver Tyrek Hill and tight end Travis Kelce at will. The Chiefs became a well-oiled offensive machine, and Patrick was named the NFL's Most Valuable Player. Patrick had decided not to participate in any endorsement deals until he had proven himself on the NFL field and established a charitable foundation.

Yet even as he ascended rapidly into the football elite, and all the endorsement deals and media pressure that accompany it, he remained grounded and concerned with the welfare of others. This quality has allowed him to be a natural team leader and a pillar of the Kansas City community. No matter how much people love Patrick on the field, they also love his caring heart and concern for others off the field. Patrick has stayed true to his Texas roots, conveying a sense of courtesy and respect. Patrick would say yes, sir in our discussions. I asked him to call me Leigh because we would be working closely together, to which he responded, "Yes, sir."

Not even ten years into the NFL, Patrick already has a bonanza of accolades and highlights to his name. He has three championship rings and has proven himself a once-in-a-generation talent. Patrick Mahomes' ascent into the NFL accelerated the growth of Steinberg Sports and Entertainment Agency. My son Matt was performing well. Selwyn Roberts was a master of social media posting. Julia Faron, a valued Rams public relations expert, came aboard to run our press interactions. Ian Hill morphed from being an excellent assistant to being an administrative executive. We had started to build an infrastructure based on campus contacts and the friends and family of our clients. We were now in a place to attract the top players in the country. We spent less time searching for new clients and more time working with our current roster.

That's why it's so important to network and brand yourself because, eventually, the opportunities will come to you. When you encounter a wall, don't be deterred; there's always a way over, around, or through. There is always a way forward, even if it's not immediately apparent, even if you have to dig deep and rely on the qualities that have always served you well, even in your darkest days.

Chapter 10

Generosity: Be a Change Agent

In 1960, the Steinberg family piled into their 1956 Plymouth station wagon, equipped with push-button gearshifts, and headed on a cross-country trip across the United States. We visited thirty states. The family trip was filled to the brim with great memories, but I'll never forget what occurred in downtown Chicago.

While stopping at a store, our family witnessed a violent altercation between a man and a woman. This man was attacking the woman in broad daylight, and a small crowd had formed to watch, but no one intervened. No one, except my dad. He got out of the car and demanded that the man leave the woman alone. I watched in amazement with my face pressed against the window, in awe of my dad's heroic act. Much later, I realized that we'd witnessed a pimp assaulting his prostitute, but it made no difference to my dad. Many talk about the need for action but rarely stand up when it is their time to act. When a problem arises in the world, whether it's as minor as picking up trash or as significant as fighting racism and climate change, the human tendency is to assume that someone else will address it. Why step in when we can wait for the amorphous "They" or "Them" to fix the problem at hand? We stand by in the hopes that older individuals, business leaders, or political figures will take on the hard work. But it rarely happens this way.

My father would often look at me and say, “If you wait for others to take responsibility and improve conditions, you could wait forever. The ‘they’ is ‘you’, son.” It was an echo of Gandhi’s famous mantra, “Be the change you wish to see in the world.” My father instilled in me a responsibility to make a difference in the world. I understood that, in order to make real change, you have to be committed to being a part of the execution of the change.

Generosity, giving back, is also part of your comeback journey. When you’re bruised and battered, it might seem like you have nothing to offer to the world, or like you don’t have the capacity. And to be fair, when you’re really at your lowest point, you might be justified in being more of a “taker” than a “giver.” But once you find your footing and you’re on your way back to the top, you will discover that healing and restoring yourself necessitates sharing your gifts with others. That reinforces your metamorphosis and helps ratify the lessons you’ve learned. Spread the light that shines within you. And show gratitude for the help you received along the way by practicing altruism and self-sacrifice in the service of others. Who knows? You might even play the role of savior in someone else’s comeback, too.

I like the term "change agent"—one who not only improves himself or herself but catalyzes change in others. Around our dinner table, my father constantly emphasized that it was our responsibility to become change agents. Change agents champion organizations and people in their efforts to improve the human condition. They take action to find solutions. They inspire, influence, and invigorate.

My brothers and I grew up believing we could make a difference. That we could help administer significant change by utilizing our knowledge and our ability to communicate across racial, financial, and political barriers. My father taught us that, even though change often comes slowly, giving up on the mission wasn't an option. In my life, I had constantly helped others, but when I had lost control to drinking, I had also lost my capacity to give.

Now that I was racking up sober days like Aikman used to rack up TDs, it was time to take a hard look at how I could give back, perhaps in altogether new ways.

My comeback has led me to focus directly on making a difference on several fronts. One was simply working with a new pool of clients and advocating on their behalf. Another was using my own influence in the sporting world to mobilize others to support social and charitable causes. I also had the opportunity to play a role in making collision sports safer (more on that later), and I have researched and promoted new health and productivity modalities (also the subject of a later chapter). I'm incredibly passionate about each of these areas and the impact this can have on developing, improving, and saving lives.

Throughout my life, I have spent a lot of time working alongside amazing organizations to create a blueprint for peace. The secret ingredient in this endeavor is the younger generation. Of course, the youth are our future, so training and preparing them to be the change that we all want to see makes all the sense in the world to me. I was also inspired by my brother Jim's journey as a seeker of higher truth and enlightenment. Jim and I have taken very different paths, though we have each found a way to make an impact. Far from the glitzy world of A-list athletes, Jim is a devoted follower of an Eastern spiritual leader known as Da Free John. He found peace and fulfillment in their meditation practice, which has inspired him to give speeches and write books on living an enlightened, spiritually pure life.

My other brother, Donald, dedicated his life to working for the State Department and NGOs to help people in need around the world. As an ambassador to Angola, he worked hard (albeit unsuccessfully) to broker a peace accord between the government and the rebel leader Jonas Savimbi. He was voted most courageous diplomat in the State Department for that effort. He was President Bill Clinton's expert on African policy, was special envoy to troubled Haiti, and desperately urged intervention by the United States to stop the genocide in Rwanda. Donald was a leader at USAID and later became the United States Ambassador to the World Landmine Commission. Landmines are a scourge that kill and maim people (often children) around the world, sometimes years or decades after an armed conflict has ended. It costs $30,000 to de-mine an acre, a laborious process. But thanks to the efforts of my brother and others in the commission, hundreds of landmines were removed in places like Angola, Mozambique, and Cambodia. Even though Donald was high up in government, he was mostly an unsung hero. Few members of the public know him by name, let alone his work. But that's how most heroes are: good people who contribute, in however small ways, to a collective action. Their individual efforts might be as small as a drop of water, but a million drops make an ocean.

There are unsung heroes everywhere. Parents who tend to, love, and shape their children to the best of their ability. Teachers who forgo working in corporate America, swallow a low paycheck, and still strive to prepare the next generation. Nurses, firefighters, doctors, and police officers all risk their lives to help others—selfless individuals who dedicate their time to working in charity organizations. Even the everyday clerk who assists individuals in the checkout line is providing a public good. These people power our society and work ceaselessly to make things better, with or without recognition. I've tried to spur change by leveraging my position in the sports world. Sports tend to be a meeting ground for big business, big politics, and big entertainment. These people are not inherently humanitarian workers, but they are often willing to put their resources and influence behind worthy causes. My career has allowed me to communicate not only with players but also with team owners, head coaches, political officeholders, and corporate CEOs. The confluence of these powerful communities offers real possibilities for the greater good.

As you rebuild the foundation of your life, take a moment to look at whatever area of work you're in, and figure out how you can become an agent of change in that part of your life. What is your purpose? How can you infuse that purpose to bring forth better outcomes? If getting back into your groove means re-opening your small business or advocating for issues in your local community, what can you do? How can you better your life as well as the lives of others? Meaningful change takes patience and resiliency. But as you heal others, you will heal yourself, too.

FIGHTING FOR ATHLETES

I owe my success to the athletes I've represented. Without sports stars, agents aren't going to get very far in their careers! But it becomes a mutual partnership; together, you rise to the top.

That is the nature of the agent's job: you advocate fiercely on their behalf. When I graduated from law school, I was looking for a career that would allow me to make an impact. I'll never forget arriving in Atlanta in 1975 with my first client, Steve Bartkowski, to find a sea of people pressed up against police tape, their hands reaching out in hopes of touching Steve. Klieg lights were flashing in the sky, and the first thing we heard was a TV reporter covering the arrival saying, "We interrupt the late news to bring you a special news bulletin. Steve Bartkowski and his attorney Leigh Steinberg have just arrived at the Atlanta Airport, and we will switch you live for an in-depth interview."

This is when I realized that athletes are admired by many fans, much like movie stars, achieving celebrity status and holding the public's attention. It was clear that their high profile could trigger positive imitative behavior, especially among younger people. When I began my career, it was the wild, wild west of sports agents. There was no guaranteed right to agent representation. In 1975, another brilliant client came my way: Pat McInally, a punter and wide receiver who the Cincinnati Bengals drafted. He also had the all-time highest score on the Wonderlic IQ test.

When I called Bengals President and General Manager Mike Brown to begin negotiations, he hung up on me. Some franchises simply refused to communicate with an agent representing a player. This system was broken and in need of reform. I wanted to develop a different model for representing athletes, treating them not simply as financial clients but holistically, focusing on how to fulfill their needs. This started with carefully listening to the values and priorities each player expressed individually. I sought not only to enhance their athletic careers but also to lay a foundation for an exciting life after pro sports.

Usually, sports agents find an athlete, sign them to a representation contract, and then hungrily look for the next athlete and the next paycheck. I didn't want to follow that path. Instead, I tried to shift my mindset to being an agent of change for the athletes I represented. What if we viewed the NFL, NBA, MLB, and NHL as just the first step and not the ultimate goal? Athletes can't compete forever, and in the NFL and its equivalent in other leagues, the average career is actually pretty short. We have to think about how their (often brief) time at the top could serve as a springboard for the next stage.

The first day I talk to an athlete about representation, I ask them what skills, interests, or passions they have outside of sports. We teach them how to network with businessmen who could serve as mentors for their second career. Networking involves being out and about in the community and training to attend banquets and events with charitable foundations. It's the ability to walk up to someone the athlete doesn't know, engage them in a brief discussion, and collect their card. On the back of the card, we ask the athlete to write a physical description of the person and any details about them they can remember. That helps the athlete put together a powerful contact list to nurture. We also encourage our athletes to use the off-season as an opportunity to work in a business or develop a skill that could plant a seed for their future.

For example, we explore how athletes can be public figures who champion a cause. This is good for the athlete and the public. Fans (and young fans in particular) tune out authority figures. They might not listen to their parents, teachers, or law enforcement personnel. But when a macho figure like heavyweight champion Lennox Lewis cuts a public service announcement stating, "real men don't hit women," children listen. A voice like Lennox Lewis can trigger positive imitative behavior, especially in rebellious adolescents. In a similar vein, boxer Oscar De La Hoya and quarterback Steve Young cut a public service announcement—"prejudice is foul play"—that promoted tolerance.

Television brings the profiles and visages of professional athletes into homes across the country in a larger-than-life way. Our world's athletes hold the ears of the general public, regardless of age. They are at the top of the food chain.

I make it a priority that our clients recognize the power they hold, because many professional athletes do not. As they move into the starter position, their fanbase and reach grow. Overnight, they become role models, regardless of whether or not they're up for the task. When I approach new clients, we aren't just talking endorsements, contracts, and salary caps. I ask how I can help them use their platform for good. I encourage athletes to return to the communities that helped shape them. In their hometowns, they could establish a scholarship fund at their high school or work with a church or Boys and Girls Club. In their college towns, I suggest that they return to their alma mater and establish a scholarship or endow a weight room or academic classroom. I have challenged them to find a problem or illness that particularly bothers them and set up a charitable foundation to deal with the issue. They could put together an advisory committee to support the foundation, using leading business professionals, political figures, and community leaders to help support the program. My athletes, collectively with their contributions and fundraising, have raised well over a billion dollars.

MERLIN OLSEN

The charitable side of my comeback took an unexpected turn when I was called to serve as an expert witness in high-profile trials. This was a way to use my lifetime of specialized knowledge to fight for justice, not only for the litigants in the particular case, but also for others who would be affected by the outcome. I served as an expert witness in cases where an athlete was the victim of medical malpractice or exposed to unfair practices that led to their death or inability to succeed in their sport. While I was in early recovery, I was asked by a talented lawyer and litigator, Denise Clancy, from a prestigious Dallas law firm, to get involved in the Merlin Olsen court case. This case refocused me on the many dimensions of player health and safety, and on my continuing responsibility to innovate and pioneer better practices.

Merlin Olsen was a standout defensive tackle who played for fifteen seasons with the Los Angeles Rams. I rooted for him as a young Rams fan. He was part of the defensive line nicknamed the "Fearsome Foursome." While he struck terror into offenses all over the league, off the field, he was warm and charming, with a deep, mellifluous voice.

Merlin's dominance on the field earned him an induction into the Pro Football Hall of Fame in 1982. After his pro career ended, he went on to become an announcer, an actor, and a spokesperson for a variety of companies. You might remember him being on a hit television show in the seventies and eighties called The

Little House on the Prairie, and also having his own show called Father Murphy. He was also the leading spokesman for Florists' Transworld Delivery (FTD). But while he should have been enjoying his retirement in comfort, a devastating health crisis changed everything. He was diagnosed with mesothelioma, a rare and aggressive form of cancer that develops in the lining of the body's internal organs. In 2009, he filed suit against various companies for having caused the illness as a result of asbestos exposure, but he didn't survive long enough to see it to the end. In 2010, Merlin died.

The suit proceeded, nonetheless. There were thousands of others whose bodies had been poisoned by asbestos, in part because of the negligence of companies that used the deadly material. This was a major issue. But getting justice was an uphill battle. Merlin's attorneys would first have to establish that the defendant's negligence created liability. The case centered around the issue of liability, whether or not the attorneys could prove that the companies were responsible for his getting mesothelioma. I'd been brought into the Merlin Olsen case as an expert witness on the issue of his potential future earnings. My task was to put together a "what-if scenario."

If he hadn't been robbed of his life, what would he have gone on to accomplish? And how would that translate into specific lost earnings? With Merlin's passing, I felt it was my duty to do the best I could to honor his potential accomplishments based on his past achievements. I also wanted his family to finally find some comfort in knowing that his wishes to see the case through would be honored. Merlin knew his case could potentially help someone else and even save lives.

I prepared a comprehensive package that illustrated Merlin's potential earnings across a variety of categories. Merlin was sixty-nine when he died, but he was a Hall of Fame athlete and a talented actor. Many people loved his personality and generosity. I'm sure that if it weren't for his illness, he would have continued to work in Hollywood or would have had a role in NFL broadcasts. What is effective in these cases is finding comparable athletes in a similar age group and profile to serve as a comparison. One clear comparison to Olsen was the iconic Joe Namath, a professional quarterback who played for the New York Jets and the Los Angeles Rams. Namath continued to appear in endorsements in his seventies.

I made sure all of these details were in my presentation, which enumerated all the endorsements, public speaking engagements, books, and coaching gigs that Olsen could have prospered from. After my deck was completed, I gave it to the attorneys so they could include it in the pretrial discovery process. Discovery, which consists of written interrogatories and in-person depositions, is designed to give both parties enough information to settle without going to court. With no agreement following the interrogatories, we went straight to the deposition phase of the case.

If you haven't taken part in a deposition, it is a grueling cross-examination by the opposing attorney. Depositions allow opposing attorneys to ask as many questions about the testimony as they want, for as long as they want. Being the witness can be torturous, and staying focused requires hours of intense concentration. Unlike the movies and TV shows, where there are many commercial breaks or cuts in the action, in a deposition, there are few. Like draft time, every second seems like a minute, and every minute seems like an hour. The defendant's counsel is hoping you will state something that later turns out to be untrue or inconsistent. But I knew Merlin deserved better, so I made sure I did my best to be as detailed as possible so that his truth was presented with facts.

The deposition was exhausting, lasting seventeen hours over two days. At the end, the opposing attorney looked me dead in the eyes and asked, “Mr. Steinberg, how do we know that any of your projections are based on reality?

It defies common sense to think that a seventy-year-old man would want to be involved in all of these activities. What proof do you have that Mr. Olsen would participate in any of this?”

The deposition room was deafeningly silent as I stared right back at the stoneface attorney grilling me. “Well, that’s simple,” I said in a matter-of-fact tone. “In 2006, I gave the presenting speech for my client, Warren Moon, as he was inducted into the Pro Football Hall of Fame in Canton, Ohio. I accompanied him to the luncheon attended by all previous inductees. I ended up sitting between Olsen and Moon. Merlin asked me a series of questions about whether I could help him continue as a broadcaster and commercial endorser.”

The opposing attorney looked at me, stunned for a moment. In his silence, the people in the hearing room realized his mistake and knew that he had just completely validated Merlin’s intentions and my projections. After a long pause, he stated, "No more questions." Realizing the effect that my testimony would have on a jury at a later trial was a major factor in the opposing attorney's decision to settle the case quickly. Denise Clancy had done a brilliant job in establishing liability. I also testified in a case involving a Grambling State basketball player who tragically died from heat prostration after being punished with hours of running in sweltering heat. The trial took place in an old courthouse in Shreveport, Louisiana, surrounded by Confederate Civil War figures. I had to connect with a Southern jury. We did well enough that the college settled soon after.

Hall of Famer and beloved San Diego Padres player Tony Gwynn's death was linked to the chewing tobacco sold by the company. I felt deeply moved by his incredible talent for hitting and his upbeat, gregarious personality. So, I prepared a report for the wrongful death suit. I also testified in Kansas City at the wrongful death trial of my cherished client, Kansas City Chiefs linebacker Derrick Thomas. His untimely death occurred when his truck overturned on an icy road, and the suit was filed against the car company that manufactured his vehicle.

Chapter 11

New Ventures

The sports business continues to develop in new fields and manifestations, including some you might not normally associate with it, such as art. But I have always thought that sports provide a rich source of artistic expression. I have become partners with a gifted artist named Mike Sullivan. Mike's talents span murals, painting, and the creation of collectables and memorabilia. I was impressed by a wonderful mural he did of baseball player Jackie Robinson at UCLA's baseball stadium, and by a moving memorial mural to Pat Tillman displayed at Sun Devil Stadium in Tempe, Arizona.

Mike also produced an iconic Super Bowl quarterback painting and somehow got every winning quarterback from the first fifty Super Bowls to sign it. This is a truly iconic work. It's the only painting that these quarterbacks have signed as a group and can never be duplicated. Mike unveiled the painting, QB50, at my Super Bowl party at Salt River Fields at Talking Stick and it was on display at my thirty-eighth annual Super Bowl party in

New Orleans. Throughout my various ventures and over the years, I've been approached several times by owners who wanted me to consider serving as a top executive for their franchise. But I never acted on these offers because I loved living in Berkley and Newport Beach and the freedom and autonomy that came from having a practice with nationwide impact. My longtime partner, Jeff Moorad, was CEO of the Arizona Diamondbacks and the owner of the San Diego Padres. He told me our skill sets—understanding the athletic mentality, branding and marketing, and contract construction—were the perfect formula for running a successful franchise.

So, in the fall of 2023, I was intrigued when a group of businesspeople approached me about leading an effort to purchase a professional sports franchise. They would be responsible for raising the money. My role would be to guide them through the process and prepare for the post-sale structure and staffing of the team. My relationships with so many people in the NFL would help me understand the lay of the land.

Fortuitously, around this time, the Washington Commanders NFL franchise was put up for sale by owner Dan Snyder. The last franchise that was sold in the NFL was the Denver Broncos for $4.7 billion. The Commander's price would clearly be much more. They had national stature as one of four or five gateway teams with huge fan bases and a notable history in the NFL. The market size encompassed 6.2 million people. Yet the 2022 season averaged 59,000 fans, and their non-ticket sales revenue was the lowest in the league. So clearly, there was much room for revenue growth.

The league requirement for majority ownership is to own at least thirty percent of the team. No more than twenty-five limited partners can comprise the remaining owners. Many potential bidders were deterred by the belief that Amazon and Washington Post owner Jeff Bezos (who had by then set up a home base in Washington) would outbid anyone for the team. I believed that the fraught relationship between the Post and Dan Snyder made it unlikely that Snyder would accept an offer from Bezos. We found a prospective majority partner in Laguna Beach. We had begun to interact with Snyder's Bank of America representatives in Charlotte.

I felt we needed to make a preemptive high-opening proposal. Our group bid was six billion dollars with an additional 500 million to be paid to Snyder if the team was resold or, if not, at the end of ten years. This was a staggering bid, the largest in American sports history. But we were sure it was worth it. The NFL is bigger than ever, and the potential is immense. We wanted to grow Washington's franchise value. Six months later, the Forbes valuation of NFL franchises ranked Dallas at $10 billion and the Commanders at $6.3 billion, showing that our projection was prescient.

Not to mention, franchise values have soared throughout professional sports. In 1976, Tampa Bay and Seattle entered the NFL with a purchase price of $16.5 million. Today, the Dallas Cowboys are valued at over $12 billion, and the NBA Lakers at $10 billion. And as long as television contracts keep expanding and ancillary revenue sources keep growing, franchise prices will continue to accelerate.

However, though we had the leading bid, our project was derailed because the lead investor did not qualify. So that was that, and I never had to confront the dilemma of being an agent and a team minority owner simultaneously.

It would truly have been a dream come true to become a part-owner of a football team like Washington. It would, in some ways, complete the circle that I started back in 1975. It would also give me a position to make meaningful changes to protect athletes and to advocate for another cause of mine: giving racial minorities more say in professional football ownership and leadership.

I have represented talented athletes in a broad variety of sports. One relatively new area that is exploding is esports. There is a robust, growing market not only in player involvement but also in fan engagement and viewership. Although these fans may be gamers themselves, they are passionately watching these players perform. By 2025, the global esports audience is projected to be ~640.8 million, including ~318.1 million "enthusiasts" (roughly equivalent to frequent viewers) and ~322.7 million occasional viewers. Revenue estimates for 2025 vary by methodology and market coverage, ranging from ~$0.65 billion globally (with a narrow market definition) to upwards of $2.4 billion across G7 markets, with most analysts pointing to a multi-billion-dollar scale by the late 2020s.

These projects helped me reignite my passion and desire to make a comeback, and working in these various areas keeps me energized and connected to my dedication to making the world a better place for everyone.

SOCIETAL PROBLEMS

At this point in life, my highest priority aside from parenting is to tackle problems affecting our society. Having a hand in the nation's favorite source of entertainment has gifted me with a public platform and proximity to influential individuals. Individuals who want to be of service to others. I've always bifurcated my public profile and everyday life. Being high profile has no inherent value; its value lies in leveraging it to make a positive difference in others' lives. I'm under no illusion that newspaper clippings, acclaim, or having a building dubbed in my honor will somehow endure beyond this lifetime. Nor does being famous or successful excuse me from being a kind person—or even from my responsibility to take out the garbage every week. Self-absorption is not an option. And that's important to remember in an era of multiple, global crises that proceed unabated. One issue that ignites a fire in me is intolerance. I was not alive during the Holocaust and was too young during the Civil Rights Movement to do more than volunteer. But the problems of today are on our watch. You and I are responsible for fixing this. This is our time to show leadership and fight for a tolerant, loving spirit in our country.

In the wake of the Oklahoma City bombing, I created a program with the Anti-Defamation League of B'nai B'rith, a group that fights against hate. In the thirty largest urban areas in this country, we trained young volunteers, business leaders, and educational leaders to identify extremist groups. Then they were schooled in how to support local police departments during crises and assist local schools in teaching tolerance. The result was a nationwide battalion of volunteers pushing back against the forces of hate. I consider that one of my greatest achievements, actually.

And that program is more relevant now than ever. Currently, the bigots are on the march again. I don't want to have any young child traumatized because of their race or ethnicity. My current team is working to improve and build on what we did years ago, bringing this program back bigger and better. Everyone has an open invitation to join me on this mission.

We need to be vigilant!

As an extension of my work educating athletes and speaking on college campuses, I also saw the need to teach tolerance to the next generation of middle and high school students. We organized a program that brought together students from Orange County with diverse backgrounds: white, African, Latino, and Asian. The goal was to train a generation of students to unite people of diverse backgrounds and to teach them leadership skills. We had a melting pot of what our world looks like today, brought together for a series of summer camps. I also partnered with Rusty Kennedy and the Human Relations Commission of Orange County to do the actual teaching.

The middle schoolers went to a day camp, and the high schoolers went off for a week to summer camp in the mountains at Big Bear. They were taught various skills, including how to organize, write, and run a public service campaign. In addition to learning new skills, the most important thing was that they interacted with understanding, compassion, and respect. And then there is climate change, perhaps the biggest existential threat to our entire planet. It's certainly too big for any one nation, much less a person, to get their arms around. But because it is global and affects virtually everyone, we all need to find a way to contribute. Our children will rightfully ask us whether we knew the environment was changing and what we did to cure it.

Years ago, I created a program to deal with the reality of climate change. It was called the Sporting Green Alliance. I created a package of sustainable technologies in wind recycling, resurfacing, water, and solar panels to take to stadiums, arenas, and practice fields in sports. The goal was to reduce carbon emissions and energy costs in those venues and to establish them as teaching platforms. Millions of fans would attend games, see a waterless urinal or a solar panel, and be motivated to adopt those practices in their own homes and businesses. This would put sports in a position to stimulate positive environmental change.

If we add golf courses to stadiums, arenas, and practice fields, that is a serious amount of real estate. I would really like to resurrect this project. Ultimately, the reason I work endlessly is because I have a passion for making our world better, and if you can do something for another human being, you need to act upon that feeling. You and I are the "they" that's responsible. There's not enough time for one person to conquer all of society's ills. This is a team effort.

EDUCATION

Education is the ultimate key to thriving in our world. My grandfather was a restaurateur who owned some of the country's biggest restaurants, including the Pavillon Royal on Long Island. When he moved to LA in the thirties, he owned the Trocadero, which was frequented by movie stars. My father could have followed in his footsteps and made a fortune, too, but he turned it down because he wanted to teach young people. Deep down, every good person in this world knows the impact and importance of education.

It's not just about learning to read, write, and do math. Education is about gaining the knowledge and skills to become a better person to help advance the world we live in. It is also about people skills and learning how to get along with others in a diverse society. I received a proper education, and it has helped me grow personally and professionally. My education in school and at home made me into the man I am today. And in this last part of my life, I want to give back to people.

I want to inspire the next generation, and that's why I'm a huge proponent of education and have education as a key mission in my plans. I've combined my interest in education with my professional expertise to cultivate the next generation of sports professionals and equip them with the ethics, values, and skills they need not only to succeed financially but also to give back.

In a minute, we will get to the Agent Academy because young people are looking for a way to break into the profession. One of the things I tell people trying to reconstruct their lives or make a comeback is to find a way to distinguish themselves from the great mass of competitors. It starts with a unique resume. If I have 150 resumes on my desk, they all look somewhat similar. So, you need an approach that is creative enough to attract the employer's attention. Instantly I remember, one time I was in Waco, Texas, speaking at Baylor University. I happen to love Diet Dr. Pepper, and Waco is the home of the Dr. Pepper Hall of Fame. So, I had fun visiting the hall and talked about it on stage. Several weeks later, a bottle of Diet Dr. Pepper arrived at the office, mailed by Andrew Woodward, a creative young aspirant seeking to break into the business.

On the wrapper, it said "Established 1975," which was the year I began my practice. He replaced the usual "Established 1885" label found on every Dr. Pepper—now that is thinking outside the box! And it had a picture of Andrew next to me. The other side of the bottle listed its "nutritional info": "work ethic 100% daily requirement, creativity 100%, commitment 100%, and passion 100%." It was very clever and showed research into our history and values. We hired Andrew, who has since had a successful career in sports marketing.

In another example, a book by Dr. Seuss called All the Places You'll Go showed up in the mail. Superimposed over the wild characters in the book were pictures of me, my office, and my clients. The journey in the book started in Berkeley in 1975. At one point, it reached a crossroads, and at that juncture, it depicted me meeting a young man. He goes through the fictional journey with me, having made major contributions to the growth of our business. It was extremely creative and illustrated the exact skill set our firm was looking for. And we hired him. His name was Kris Cuaresma-Primm. He has gone on to be very successful in his career.

If you can put yourself in a prospective employer's heart and mind and figure out what they are looking for, you can make a connection.

THE AGENT ACADEMY

The Agent Academy is a training and education program we started in 2016. Since then, it has been held in person in Washington, DC; New York; Ann Arbor; Columbus; Chicago; Philadelphia; Indianapolis; Houston; Dallas; San Francisco; Berkeley; Las Vegas; and Newport Beach, as well as a few "virtual academies." The response has been great, and I truly believe we are making a difference. Our youngest attendee so far was twelve, and our oldest was seventy-three. No matter the age, we have a place for you if you are willing to learn.

The Agent Academy endeavors to teach the agent skill set and to build the next generation of ethical, principled, well-educated professionals in sports. This is my attempt to create a whole new generation that knows that they can use sports to make a difference in the world. They can use sports to make an impact. That's what I've been doing for decades, and I wish to share that knowledge with others. The academy first covers the fundamentals of establishing an agency, including the economics, regulations, required qualifications, and how to get started. We discuss ways to brand the practice and the materials needed to support it. We are honest about the financial challenges of establishing an agency and emphasize how to keep fixed costs low while maintaining high profitability.

We teach the four components of sports representation: recruiting, contract negotiations, marketing and branding, and client service. Recruiting is the most critical process because talented athletes make a talented agent. Finding talent and understanding their needs and wants is crucial. This is where your listening skills, the ability to get into the heart and mind of a young athlete and discover their true agenda, make all the difference. My ability to sign sixty-four first-round football players, thirty first-round baseball players, and a handful of NBA first-rounders rested on my ability to understand each athlete uniquely. Using real athletes and their parents, including Patrick Mahomes, Warren Moon, Mike Sherrard, and Marvell Tell, we set up agent teams to make presentations and answer questions.

This skill, the ability to present a compelling argument in a competitive environment and win over the other side, is important. Selling and recruiting clients or customers is a vital component of anyone trying to make it in the business world. We all need to master these skills. The next exercise is negotiating. Half of the participants play general managers, and half play agents. They each have common facts and unique facts on their side. They then have a player contract with many clauses and concepts to negotiate, and they need to reach an agreement on a draft pick or a veteran player.

Because many people feel uncomfortable negotiating for themselves, they can make one of two key errors in their approach. Number one, they cannot articulate their goals and what is critically important to them in a deal. They are unduly passive and agree to a deal they are immediately unhappy with. Or two, people are overly aggressive and belligerent in the interaction, which leads to almost certain deadlock. We all negotiate in our lives. Husbands and wives negotiate how to divide domestic chores and where to go on vacation. Parents negotiate with their children on issues ranging from appropriate dress and hair standards to the time of curfew. We buy automobiles, purchase homes, negotiate for our own compensation, and negotiate in business. I wrote a book, Winning with Integrity: Getting What You're Worth Without Selling Your Soul (Villard, Random House), to promote win-win negotiation. Being able to negotiate contracts between a player and a pro franchise that maximizes their compensation will help determine how many clients you can recruit. And ensure that you keep them as clients for their career.

I also feel it is important to teach our participants how to help someone, like an athlete, through a crisis. If an athlete has been involved in aberrational behavior lapses, such as drunk driving, domestic violence, or a bar fight, there is almost always press coverage. What is the best way to try to do image and relationship repair in the aftermath? We may face these issues with ourselves, or our family and friends, so the value of these lessons goes far beyond the narrow world of sports agencies.

The Agent Academy has been a great success, but there are so many more work opportunities within the sports world, and that's why we started the Sports Career Conference. The Sports Career Conference exposes young people to the various areas of sports career opportunities. We're dedicated to having a significant number of women and people of color in attendance and on the panels. We want to show everyone, even groups traditionally excluded from the world of sports management, that they have a chance to do this. In this way, we are forging a new generation of sports professionals with ethics and values that see sports as a tool for positive change. These skills will not only enhance the ability of people in crisis to make a comeback, but they are also available to all of us who simply want to improve our own lives and businesses.

When someone emerges from a great personal crisis or low point—whether it's the loss of a loved one, a health battle, addiction, financial ruin, or an emotional breakdown—rebuilding life isn't just about personal healing. It's also about re-anchoring oneself in the world, rediscovering purpose, and reestablishing connections with others. Giving back, through charity, service, or acts of altruism, is a pivotal part of this transformation. It is more than a good deed—it's a form of renewal. During a crisis, a person's world often contracts. Pain, fear, or shame can create a sense of isolation. But helping others pulls the focus outward. It reminds us that we're not alone in suffering, and it reconnects us with the broader human experience. Altruism becomes a bridge from a broken past to a future rooted in meaning. Giving also fosters a sense of agency. After a time of helplessness, taking action for someone else's benefit is profoundly empowering. It reinforces the idea that you still have value to offer, that your story, and even your scars, can be useful. This shift, from being in need to being of service, is profound.

Moreover, giving back nurtures gratitude. It transforms survival into empathy and hardship into humility. Being a change agent, one with the great power to not only alter your own life but to transform others', too, is a great gift. It turns suffering into strength, isolation into connection, and despair into opportunity. In helping others rise, we lift ourselves, as well.

ATHLETE REPRESENTATION

In my representation of Miami QB Tua Tagovailoa, I met and bonded with his amazing parents, Galu and Diane. They are exemplars of good parenting and intimately involved in Polynesian culture and heritage. Galu and Diane created an organization, Raising Champions, that trains athletes for the next level, provides life coaching and mentoring, and assists in NIL deals for almost fifty high school and college football players. I visited their facility in Alabaster, Alabama, this summer and met their talented staff. I was so inspired by the work they were doing that I joined forces with them to create a new agency, Tagovailoa Steinberg Sports, which will represent athletes in the NIL space and offer NFL representation. Daniel Myung has played a vital role in this new formation.

FILM & ENTERTAINMENT

One example of sports and entertainment intersecting is a reality show called America's Quarterback, which allows twelve aspiring quarterbacks who have never been on an NFL roster to move to Los Angeles, where they will be trained the same way we train an NFL draftee, preparing for the scouting process. There is a Hall of Fame coach, a Hall of Fame quarterback, and an agent as judges, and one quarterback is terminated each week until the winner is determined. The winner will get a tryout with an actual NFL team. There will be backstory on these athletes and their hopes and dreams. The communities they come from will be passionate supporters.

We will be able to build text messaging, sponsorship, and other ancillary revenue streams. I am partnered with producer Andrew Glassman and agent Rob Lee on this project, and I'm excited to see it come to life. Another exciting development is my work as a technical advisor on motion pictures, including a new film inspired by Irrelevant Week.

Beyond film and TV, a company that successfully blends sports and entertainment is Cameo, founded by Steven Galanis and Martin Belinco. Cameo uses video messaging to connect talent with fans and make their dreams come true. This blend is reflected not only in innovative companies but also in sports and entertainment conferences such as SEICon, hosted by my friend Shawn Garrity. As these ventures gained momentum, I started to see opportunities that extend beyond sports and entertainment—fields where the same principles of representation and advocacy could make a real difference. Working with Dr. Michael Suk reminded me that representation isn't limited to sports or entertainment.

The principles I'd relied on for decades, preparation, integrity, and advocating for people in high-pressure environments, apply in many fields. Helping talented physicians navigate contracts with hospitals, HMOs, and insurance companies showed me how far the concept could reach. That experience also opened the door to discussions about representation in the artificial intelligence and technology sectors. Leaders in those spaces face their own challenges, and many of the skills I'd developed over my career translate directly. Whether helping an athlete reach peak performance, a doctor negotiate a fair contract, or a tech innovator manage their career path, the fundamentals remain the same.

As I looked ahead, I saw that those same principles didn't stop at business. They also applied to health and wellness areas I had spent years watching athletes struggle with, often long after their playing days ended.

Chapter 12

Healthy Minds, Healthy Bodies

Health and wellness have always been central to an athlete's ability to perform. Over time, the definition of both has shifted. It's no longer just about strength or endurance. It's about recovery, long-term function, mental sharpness, and preserving the quality of life as athletes move into retirement.

Over the decades, I've represented players through victories, injuries, comebacks, and the difficult transition after the cheering stops. Those experiences forced me to take a deeper look at what protection really means for athletes, not just on the field but through the rest of their lives. One issue that has become impossible to ignore is the rising awareness of concussions and brain health.

CONCUSSIONS

Although concussions or a football injury did not directly cause the death of Merlin Olsen, his passing reminded me of the physical risks athletes face. Football impacts every part of the body, including the hips, joints, bones, muscles, and especially the brain. People often focus on the dramatic hits that cause unconsciousness. But there is another category of risk: the low-level, repetitive sub-concussive blows that occur on every play at the line of scrimmage. Offensive and defensive linemen are exposed to this constant impact thousands of times throughout high school, college, and the NFL. Modern athletes are bigger, stronger, and faster, amplifying the G-forces at contact. A lineman can finish a career with 10,000 sub-concussive blows without a single diagnosed concussion, yet the cumulative effect can mirror the damage caused by multiple knockout hits. If half the parents in America understood this, many would tell their teenage sons:

"Play any sport you want, but you cannot play tackle football."

It wouldn't end the sport overnight, but it would slowly change who participates. Football could become more of a gladiator sport, played primarily by young men with fewer economic options. Today, the neurological risks of football are widely acknowledged. Years ago, they weren't. My work representing quarterbacks who suffered repeated concussions pushed me into this issue long before it was publicly recognized. I sat in exam rooms with them, asking doctors questions they couldn't yet answer:

How many concussions are too many? What are the long-term consequences?

When should a player consider retirement?

At that time, the brain was still the last frontier of medical research. Advances in imaging, technology, and neuroscience had not yet arrived. I could not, in good conscience, continue representing players without fighting for a better understanding and better care.

PLAYER SAFETY AND CONCUSSION AWARENESS

Those early doctor visits with my players raised questions no one could answer, and it became clear we needed to bring experts together. In 1994, I organized the first Player Safety and Concussion Conference in Newport Beach. We gathered neurologists, helmet manufacturers, turf specialists, and trainers. I invited several of the quarterbacks I represented at the time, Troy Aikman, Steve Young, Warren

Moon, Drew Bledsoe, Rob Johnson, as well as linebacker Gary Plummer, to hear the presentations. We didn't walk away with many definitive answers, but we took an important step. We acknowledged that concussions existed, that sub-concussive blows were real, and that repeated head trauma had long-term effects. At that moment, simply getting the issue into the light was progress.

Not everyone saw it that way.

The NFL's medical leadership did not appreciate the attention. Dr. Elliot Pellman, who led the league's neurology committee, dismissed my efforts publicly and labeled me a "fearmonger." Some of my own clients weren't entirely comfortable, either. Players often don't want to consider long-term risks, as it disrupts their focus and challenges the mindset of toughness they've carried since childhood. Denial is woven deeply into the culture of football.

I understood their point of view, but I also knew my responsibility. As an agent, my duty extends beyond negotiating contracts. It includes protecting a player's long-term health. Getting a client top dollar means little if he cannot remember his own children at age forty.

The comparison to the military isn't far off. Athletes are trained to push through pain, recover quickly, and return to battle. I've had clients play with broken ribs, a fractured leg, and even a collapsed lung. They are conditioned to press forward, sometimes to their own detriment. I often found that parents, partners, and close friends were my strongest allies when talking to players about long-term risks. Even then, change came slowly.

By 2006, neurologists like Drs. Cantu, Bailes, Guskiewicz, Omalu, and Hovda brought national attention to the issue. They quantified what had previously been speculative: three or more concussions dramatically increase the likelihood of Parkinson's, Alzheimer's, early-onset dementia, depression, and CTE. The data confirmed what many had suspected. I called it a "ticking time bomb" and an "undiagnosed public health crisis."

To help drive awareness and research, I established the Leigh Steinberg Foundation for Concussion, Traumatic Brain Injury, and Brain Health. Our goal was to support underserved communities, raise funds for research, and elevate the conversation nationally. I believed then, and still believe, that athletes can be powerful advocates for public health. Their voices carry weight, and their personal stories can spark change.

BRAIN HEALTH SUMMIT AND BRAIN BODY LOUNGE

Over the last decade, I've incorporated brain health into my annual Super Bowl party. Working with Dr. Nicole F. Roberts, a gifted expert in neuroscience and public policy, we created the Brain Health Summit to convene leaders in medicine, sports, entertainment, media, and policy.

The Brain Body Lounge grew out of this effort, a space at the event dedicated to showcasing breakthroughs in preventive medicine, injury rehabilitation, neuroplasticity, and overall brain wellness. Dr. Roberts moderates discussions and facilitates conversations among specialists who bring forward approaches that can benefit both athletes and non-athletes. What I value most about the Summit is that it brings together perspectives from across disciplines. It's a reminder that brain health is not just a sports issue. It affects everyone, and the solutions require shared insight.

A BROADER COMMITMENT TO WELLNESS

My involvement in these initiatives has shaped my understanding of the athlete's journey. Behind every highlight reel is a human being navigating physical strain, emotional stress, and the long-term consequences of repeated impact. In representing athletes over the years, I've seen how essential it is to support them from every angle, not just financially or professionally, but also physically and mentally.

That belief guided me as I explored new approaches in the years after my own recovery from alcohol addiction. Sobriety gave me a clearer view of what health really means. It's not only the absence of illness. It's a foundation that supports every other part of life. Preventive care, longevity, and cognitive strength became areas of real interest for me, not as a doctor but as someone who wanted to understand how people can perform better and live longer, healthier lives. I began conversations with leading medical practitioners, scientists, and innovators to explore what was possible. Modern medicine in the United States tends to prioritize treatment over prevention. You seek help after symptoms appear.

But I've come to believe that the future of medicine lies in proactive care, identifying risks early, addressing inflammation before it becomes disease, and supporting the body in ways that delay decline. Advances in technology, biomedicine, and anti-aging research are accelerating quickly. The modalities emerging today have the potential to dramatically change people's lives.

My personal experience with brain health made this even more tangible. Years of alcohol abuse had taken a toll on my cognitive function, and I wanted to understand the extent of the damage. When I visited Dr. Daniel Amen and Dr. Kristen Willeumier for a SPECT brain scan, the results confirmed areas of degradation.

Their treatment regimen helped me repair those areas, and follow-up scans showed significant improvement.

Their work had such an impact on me that Kristen eventually joined the board of my foundation. My relationship with Dr. Amen has grown as well. Their expertise has been instrumental in shaping how I think about brain health, and I'm grateful for the role they've played in my recovery. My work with Dr. Amen and Dr. Willeumier opened the door to other emerging modalities. One that captured my interest was repetitive transcranial magnetic stimulation (rTMS). The process involves placing magnetic coils on the head that deliver a series of pulses to the brain. It sounds and feels a little like a rapid tapping sensation, a Woody Woodpecker rhythm on the skull, but the results were noticeable.

I'm not a physician, and I can only speak from personal experience, but rTMS struck me as a meaningful breakthrough for cognitive performance, memory, and brain recovery. I met individuals who had suffered multiple concussions, had been in comas, or were struggling with severe cognitive impairment. Many of them saw improvement through this therapy.

My curiosity led me to Brain Health Hawaii, where I met Dr. Jason Keifer and his team. They use EEG scans to track brain activity and measure progress with rTMS. I stayed in Honolulu for ten days at Dr. Keifer's second home, and during that time, I completed a series of treatments. His wife, Nicole, and their children, Koji, Elle, Nicson, and Cole, welcomed me into their routine and invited me on several family outings. Their kids called me "Uncle Leigh," which meant a great deal to me.

The EEG results showed enhanced neural processing and memory function after treatment. The improvement was significant enough that I returned for additional sessions, ultimately completing close to ninety treatments. If there were a record for the most rTMS sessions in the shortest period, I may have come close.

From Honolulu, my interest in cognitive optimization took me to Lake Nona, near Orlando, where I met with Dr. Tommy Shavers. He had developed a process called NESTRE (Neuroplasticity Strength Training). Neuroplasticity is the brain's ability to reorganize, adapt, and strengthen its neural pathways in response to internal or external stimuli. It means the brain can improve whether it's recovering from injury or seeking to operate at a higher level. Dr. Shavers, a former college athlete, suffered career-ending concussions and was told his cognitive impairments would be permanent.

He refused to accept that prognosis. Through targeted neuroplasticity work, he restored his own brain function and built the NESTRE system to help others. One aspect that stood out to me was the company's leadership. NESTRE was founded by African American former athletes whose mission is to improve people's lives through cognitive and neurological performance. Their work extends beyond sports. It applies to aging individuals, corporate leaders, students, and anyone seeking to strengthen their cognitive foundation.

During my evaluation, Dr. Shavers asked whether I was experiencing memory issues. I explained that I sometimes struggled to recall names, even of people whose careers I knew well. For example, I could see a photo of Viola Davis, and remember her filmography, name her films and television shows, but I could not immediately retrieve her name.

The team placed an image of my brain on a large screen and pointed to the region associated with facial recognition. The scan indicated suboptimal performance. For five days, I worked with their system, wearing a conductive gel and a swim-cap-like sensor array, and interacting with software designed to stimulate the targeted area. At the end of the cycle, they repeated the scan. The underperforming region was no longer flagged. While at NESTRE, I met a young man who had played college football and suffered a series of concussions that left him nearly immobilized by depression. He spent days confined to his room, unable to participate in daily life. Through training with the NESTRE team, he gradually recovered, completed his degree, earned a postgraduate degree, and eventually became a global health ambassador. His turnaround underscored what neuroplasticity can accomplish when it is applied with precision and commitment.

These experiences reinforced something important: the potential of emerging science and the impact it could have on the athletes I represent. It isn't only about treating injuries. It's about enhancing long-term cognitive strength and supporting players well after their careers end. This approach changed the way I viewed my role. Contracts and negotiations remain important, but the health and longevity of the athlete is central to their future, and to mine as their representative.

SPEEDY RECOVERY

Close games in professional sports often come down to a single moment, one drive, one possession, one sequence that determines the outcome. In those situations, the difference between winning and losing can be extremely small. I wanted to know whether there were ways athletes could enhance performance legally, without banned substances, to sharpen focus, increase energy, and recover faster. If there were safe, science-based methods that helped players be at their best in critical moments, I wanted to understand them.

My research led me to explore advances in health and wellness that could support athletes' recovery. One of the first modalities I tried was hyperbaric oxygen therapy, which I found in my own backyard at O2 Health Labs in Newport Beach. Mark Westaway and John Parks, both experts in this field, run the clinic. A hyperbaric session involves lying in a comfortable pressurized chamber for fifty minutes while breathing concentrated oxygen. There is a television mounted above the chamber, so I passed the time binge-watching The Crown, How to Get Away with Murder, The Blacklist, and even Tiger King. The sessions were not difficult, and the effects were noticeable.

Oxygen is a key factor in tissue repair and cellular function. One of the most significant findings about hyperbaric therapy is its impact on telomeres. Telomeres are the protective caps on the ends of chromosomes. Telomere length is closely associated with aging. As they shorten, cellular function declines, increasing the likelihood of age-related disease.

Stress, inflammation, poor diet, and lack of exercise all contribute to telomere shortening. A study from Israel, Hyperbaric Oxygen Therapy Increases Telomere Length and Decreases Immunosenescence in Isolated Blood Cells (Hachmo et al., 2020), found that forty sessions could lengthen telomeres by twenty percent and that sixty sessions could extend them even further. The implication is that hyperbaric oxygen therapy may slow aspects of biological aging.

Over time, I completed more than 250 sessions. Each session left me feeling mentally clearer and physically stronger. Another oxygen-based modality I explored is the Bimini NanoJet oxygen perfusion system. It uses ultrafine nanobubbles that penetrate the skin and deliver oxygen directly into soft tissue. This promotes recovery, reduces inflammation, and enhances overall wellness. I use the system daily at home. I also incorporated a tool called NanoVi, introduced to me by Dr. Rowena Gates. NanoVi supports the body's natural protein repair processes through a humidified airstream that improves cellular water function. Developed by engineer Hans Eng, the device enhances the environment in which proteins operate, helping with regeneration, stress management, energy, immune function, and performance. NanoVi is drug-free and legal for athletes. In my experience, it is a valuable part of a recovery regimen.

At O2 Labs, I also used red light therapy. The process involves lying between two LED light panels that stimulate ATP production, the energy currency of the cell. The treatment reduces internal inflammation and speeds healing. Many athletes use red light therapy to recover from injuries more quickly. At the risk of exposing the depths of my vanity, I'll admit that red light therapy also supports collagen production, which contributes to healthier skin and improved texture.

From light therapy, I moved to exploring the role of smell in brain health. Although many people consider smell the least important sense, it is the only one directly connected to the brain's memory and emotional centers. Research has shown that diminished smell stimulation can weaken memory, increase depression risk, and even signal earlier mortality. More than 160 diseases are associated with smell loss.

There is encouraging research showing that olfactory enrichment, the deliberate stimulation of smell receptors, can improve cognitive health. A study from UC Irvine found that daily exposure to a rotating set of forty scents significantly improved memory in older adults. The challenge is consistency; most people will not use dozens of individual scents twice a day. A device called Memory Air creates that consistency. It releases rotating scents while a person sleeps, making olfactory enrichment effortless. These treatment protocols showed me something straightforward: when we support the body's natural processes, it responds. Whether through oxygen, light, scent, or cellular water, the goal is the same: to reduce inflammation, enhance recovery, and improve long-term health.

STEM CELLS AND REGENERATIVE APPROACHES

As I explored different modalities to support brain and body recovery, I became increasingly interested in regenerative medicine, particularly stem cell therapy. My first experience with stem cells came through Dr. Phillip Yoo in Newport Beach. He treated a broken toe and sciatica-related back pain by injecting low-level stem cells into the affected areas. The treatment eased the discomfort in my L4 and L5 discs without surgery.

I also received stem cell injections in my temples from another practitioner to improve vision. By the end of the session, I no longer needed glasses for distance. In the United States, only limited forms of stem cell therapy are permitted due to regulations, so the treatments available domestically tend to be low-dose.

Dr. Yoo suggested I consider culture-expanded mesenchymal stem cells, which are among the purest and most potent forms available worldwide. He recommended the facility he believed to be the best, and he joined me on the trip to receive treatment himself. That brought us to Medellín, Colombia, where the U. S.-based company BioXcellerator operates its flagship clinic. Although Medellín still carries the reputation of its past, it is now a modern and beautiful city. At the clinic, I was given the bioXcellerator sports recovery protocol, which included ozone therapy, cryotherapy, hyperbaric oxygen, and supportive treatments alongside a dose of 240 million stem cells. I also received an intrathecal injection that delivered stem cells directly into my spinal cord and, subsequently, my brain.

My most recent stem cell experience has been with Dr. Michael Chan, a pioneer in the field with clinics in forty-six locations worldwide. He has authored multiple books on stem cell breakthroughs, and together we co-wrote a book about stem cells and concussions, scheduled for release in 2026. Dr. Chan treated me with stem cells in my back and knees, and the improvement has exceeded what I experienced with other therapies.

During this period, I was also introduced to Placenta Derived Protein Complex (PDPC) through Dr. Adam Sewell in Texas. PDPC includes bioactive proteins, cytokines, growth factors, and microRNAs extracted from the human placenta after childbirth. These components support tissue repair, reduce inflammation, and may help regulate immune responses. I continue to be encouraged by the early results and look forward to seeing how PDPC develops as part of regenerative medicine.

THE NEXT WAVE

Many of the treatments I explored, from oxygen-based, light-based, scent-based, to regenerative, are not yet widely accessible. They require specialized equipment, trained practitioners, or international travel. Still, I believe that many of these approaches will become mainstream in the years ahead. Athletes have already begun incorporating them into their routines, whether through home hyperbaric units, red-light beds, or trips abroad for stem cell treatment.

Seeing these results firsthand has motivated me to bring these technologies into professional and collegiate athletic programs. If these methods can support recovery and long-term health for elite athletes, they can also benefit everyday people. When I was younger, my idea of someone in their seventies was an old man sitting on a park bench feeding pigeons, wearing mismatched socks and waiting out the day. When I turned seventy-three, I realized my earlier picture had been completely wrong. I wasn't frail. I wasn't slowing down. With the help of a dedicated trainer, Tony Lattimore, I committed to three rigorous sessions a week and a daily goal of 15,000 steps. Tony is a talented trainer with a sharp sense of humor, and his support has been essential.

American culture tends to overlook the value of older adults, even when those individuals have the wisdom and experience of a lifetime. Other countries embrace aging differently, and I believe we can learn from that. For many of us in the Baby Boomer generation, these years can be among our most productive, but only if we take care of ourselves.

It is never too late to change course. No matter the damage that has already been done, physically or emotionally, there is always potential for improvement. Recovery of any kind, personal, professional, or physical, requires consistency and commitment. Showing up day after day with intention and focus makes all the difference. Each step toward better health brings you closer to a stronger, more capable version of yourself. The opportunity for a comeback is always there, and the effort is always worth it.

VICTORY LAP

The discipline I applied to my own health carried into my work. Clarity, consistency, and long-term thinking helped me stay grounded as an agent. Even as I learned about new technologies and wellness practices, the core principles I relied on throughout my career continued to guide me. They shaped the way I engaged with players, negotiated on their behalf, and approached the next chapter of my professional life.

SUPERBOWL LIV

2019 was the exact opposite of 2010, the year I had to move back into my mother's house, the year things finally and fully spiraled out of hand. But by 2019, I had bounced back. Recalling where I had been in 2010 was poignant.

In the 2019 NFL season, I watched my clients persevere through the victories and the defeats that come with playing the game of football. That year, one of my clients reached the pinnacle of an NFL player, playing in Super Bowl LIV. For me, Super Bowl weekend is one of the best weekends of the year.

On February 1, 2020, I woke up in sunny Miami, Florida, adrenaline pumping through my veins. I could not wait to leave my hotel room and head off to the festivities of the day. There are three especially iconic events in the life of a sports agent. One represents the first player selected number one in the NFL Draft. That had happened in eight separate years. Another was having clients inducted into the Pro Football Hall of Fame, which I had experienced twelve times. And the last was having a quarterback play in the Super Bowl.

I had that with the Patriots' Tony Eason and Drew Bledsoe, the Giants' Kerry Collins, and the Steelers' Neil O'Donnell; to that, you might add having your quarterback win Super Bowl MVP. That had happened three times with the Cowboys' Troy Aikman, once with the 49ers' Steve Young, and with the Pittsburgh Steelers' quarterback Ben Roethlisberger. It was about to happen again with NFL MVP Patrick Mahomes. That year, the Kansas City Chiefs faced off against the San Francisco 49ers. The countdown to kickoff had already begun, and the entire country was waiting with anticipation. Neither team had won a Super Bowl in the twenty-first century, and Kansas City hadn't won in fifty years. Both teams were hungry.

Early that morning, my Steinberg Sports staff was already working at the venue, preparing for the Super Bowl party that we would all attend. Since then, my Super Bowl parties have become a tradition, an institution. And as you know, it's not just revelry. It's charity, togetherness, community, and putting a positive face on pro sports.

And we were excited to see the fireworks Mahomes was bound to ignite come kickoff. The year before, when he won the NFL MVP award, he had a crushing loss in the AFC Championship game against Tom Brady and the New England Patriots. But now, he was in the big game and felt that this was his moment. Do kids sleep the night before Christmas? Can players truly get a restful night before Draft Day or the Super Bowl? Do you spend eight hours watching your clock the night before your exotic vacation? After a sleepless and restless night, it was finally time for me to prepare to go to the big game. On game day, some of my agents and I ended up in the Community Bank Box to watch the game. We were accompanied by Brittany, Patrick's soon-to-be wife, his mother Randi, who was proudly wearing a shirt that read "Quarterback Producer," Patrick's dad Pat, and other family members. When I stepped out of the box for a moment during the game, a flood of celebrities surrounded our box, including Jamie Foxx and Cedric the Entertainer. We had a great time mixing and mingling before the game.

For the next four hours, we watched as Patrick played dazzling football, keeping us on our toes the entire game. It was a legendary performance. When the game ended and the Chiefs were announced as the winners, chaos erupted! The Kansas City Chiefs had won the Super Bowl for the first time in fifty years. Randi began to cry. Brittany dashed out of the box to rush to the field and celebrate with Patrick. The entire stadium erupted in applause and celebration. In the past I had passes that allowed me to get down to the field and congratulate our clients, but this time I sat back. I watched Patrick accept the game's MVP award and give a speech as overwhelming emotions washed over me. He was now the thirty-third NFL starting quarterback to win a Super Bowl and the twenty-second to be named MVP of the game. That's a huge accomplishment, an iconic tradition begun with the first Super Bowl in 1967.

Patrick didn't have to say a word. His illuminating smile said it all—he was at the top of the mountain. The long-suffering Chiefs had found a spark with Patrick and reached the pinnacle of NFL success by winning the Super Bowl. Patrick's gameplay that day mirrored my past couple of years. He had a vibrant early performance. The 49ers took over the lead, and, at a ten-point deficit, 49er fans started to see victory as inevitable. Patrick and his team stayed focused and pulled off a dramatic, come-from-behind win. The Chiefs fanbase is legendary and lives and dies with their team. Everywhere I went throughout the country, there were Chiefs fans. They dress in red on Friday during football season. And the crowd noise in Arrowhead Stadium is deafening.

It was an unforgettable day for the Mahomes family, for all his teammates, for every single person in the stadium, and for me—a comeback for the ages, sixteen years in the making. The stark contrast of where I was in 2010 and how high I was sitting now was overwhelming. Since that day, Patrick has gone on to appear in four more Super Bowls, winning two and earning Super Bowl MVP honors in both victories, and signing the richest contract in sports history at the time. He won another regular-season MVP two years later and has continued to grow his charitable efforts off the field with Fifteen and the Mahomies Foundation. It has been nothing short of an honor to represent Patrick throughout this journey.

My whole career has been dedicated to helping clients beat the odds. To even make it to the NFL, much less be a starting QB or Super Bowl MVP, is a million-to-one shot. My life has also followed the same improbable pattern. But then there was something I never believed would be possible—another chance with the love of my life. One early spring afternoon, I got an unexpected call from someone from my past.

It was Amy Stoody.

We hadn't spoken in a long time. The last time we saw each other, I was at rock bottom; in fact, her understandable choice to leave me was the very thing that knocked me down to the nadir. In the intervening years, she met someone else, they got married, and that epoch of my life was sealed shut forever.

Or so I thought.

The beauty of comebacks is that they open up possibilities that you could scarcely imagine. They give you back hope. They give you a future. On the phone, she told me that she had divorced her husband. Would I like to get together in a no-pressure, no-expectations kind of way?

You bet I would.

We met for coffee and a walk on the pier. We had both changed, and yet, we were still the same. The qualities I had loved in her—her vivacity, her intelligence, her sense of humor, her compassion—burned as brightly as ever. The things she had liked in me were able to shine through again, now that I was sober, healthy, and clear-headed. We made plans to meet again. One encounter led to another. Dinners, walks, movies. But we were taking it slow. I've always been cautious at the start of a relationship, and now even more so, given our history and the fragility of starting over.

Our resurrected friendship blossomed into a courtship. The courtship bloomed into a relationship. And that relationship has matured into a melding of two hearts, a reunion of soulmates, and I asked her to marry me in July of 2025. It's been gratifying to see where my comeback has led me. I know alcoholism may not be the villain in your story. Perhaps it's a desperate fight against drug addiction, the tugging pain of heartache, the cloud of depression that refuses to leave, a crippling fear that renders you incapacitated, or overwhelming financial woes. Whatever the crisis, the world is sitting at the metaphorical edge of your father's bed, unsure how to move on. But if there is anything you can pull from my story, it's that there's a light at the end of this tunnel. Never give up or think there's no way out.

There's a speech by President Theodore Roosevelt called the "Man in the Arena" that my father put on the wall in my bedroom to inspire me. It is an apt summation of why resilience is so critical: why the ability to fail and rise again like the phoenix empowers us to get through any crisis.

"It is not the critic who counts; not the man who points out how the strong man stumbles, or where the doer of deeds could have done them better. The credit belongs to the man who is actually in the arena, whose face is marred by dust and sweat and blood; who strives valiantly; who errs, who comes short again and again, because there is no effort without error and shortcoming; but who does actually strive to do the deeds; who knows great enthusiasms, the great devotions; who spends himself in a worthy cause; who at the best knows in the end the triumph of high achievement, and who at the worst, if he fails, at least fails while daring greatly, so that his place shall never be with those cold and timid souls who neither know victory nor defeat."

I remember Jim Valvano's 1993 ESPY speech. "Don't give up. Don't ever give up," he said. Here was a man who died two weeks later but refused to stop the fight. Cancer might have killed the man, but cancer did not kill his message. His words encouraged a generation back then and continue to encourage people now. For myself, I'm living proof that the sun does rise tomorrow and that we all have inner strength to do the most impossible things.

If it wasn't for me finally coming to terms with my addiction and deciding that I was going to beat it, who knows where I might be today? I do know that creating a plan for my comeback, actively listening to people around me, remembering what was important to me, and most of all opening up to others that I needed help saved my life.

It all began with that moment on my father's bed. Reconnecting with my roots, tapping into the core values I had been taught. Resilience. Courage. Patience. Generosity. And all the other "pillars" that brought me back.

Through resiliency, reflection, and remembering my dad's wisdom, I've rediscovered the voice I once lost. A voice that spoke loudest to me at the deepest point of my fall from grace. Facing the reality of your situation and understanding you need help is the best way to start your journey to recovering from substance abuse, marital or romantic breakup, a bad decision, loss of a job, or dealing with the death of a loved one. The list goes on. My advice to anyone is to use your voice to ask for help and stop denying the tears inside you by refusing to show others that you are hurting or need help.

Looking back on those times, I wish I had listened to the people around me sooner. I wish I had recognized the hurt I was causing them as they stood by my side and did their best to support me. Most people have an inner circle in their lives that truly cares about them. Those are the people who couldn't care less if you are rich or famous—they love you for your authentic self. As I withdrew into the cocoon of denial and isolation, I started to lose touch with those people in my life. Patience will give you the fortitude to endure. Making a comeback from the depths of despair is a long game, not an overnight project. Recovery will not happen overnight; it is a day-by-day journey. Sometimes in life, we need to sit on the bench to gain a broader perspective on what lies ahead in the game. Use this time wisely to reflect and gain insight so this can be your epiphany or intervention.

Courage grants you the strength to try, to face your demons head-on, to kill the voices of self-doubt and the doubt of others. We cannot expect to do it without fear. Courage is not fearlessness, but the power to act despite your fear. Hope is the wind beneath our wings; when we falter, when we stumble, when the task seems overwhelming, we must not yield our optimism. That's precious and vital. It helps to have perspective. The very fact that others have struggled and persevered gives us strength, and when we think about it, our problems aren't so immense in the cosmic scale of things. Accountability keeps us on track. We stay accountable to others and, most of all, to ourselves, ensuring we're sticking to a plan and making progress toward a goal.

All great comebacks are journeys of two steps forward, one step back—sometimes way back. If we are resilient, we can endure hardship, struggle, pain, and doubt. Adaptability keeps us nimble, active, and able to think on our feet. The path back to the summit is rarely the same one that got you there the first time. You must blaze a new trail. Being flexible carries you through. And as you blaze that trail, remember, don't do it alone.

Giving back reaffirms our humanity, restores our agency, and helps correct the karmic balance of the universe. Your generosity might also aid someone else's comeback, whether you realize it or not. And finally, there is no victory without a sound body. Treat your body well. It's the only one you've got.

Above all else, remember resilience needs to be combined with a sense of optimism. You have to keep believing that there is light at the end of the tunnel. You have to put the obstacles of fear and frustration behind you and focus on a brighter tomorrow. Try and overcome the setbacks of rebuilding and focus on how good your life can be. No matter how bleak the road or how long the hike up the mountain is, your comeback is worth the climb.

And I leave you with this. The world doesn't need more perfection—it needs more people willing to show up as they are. Your story, no matter how broken it feels, might be the very lifeline someone else needs to keep going. You don't have to be famous or rich to make an impact. Sometimes, all it takes is a kind word, a listening ear, or the courage to tell your truth. Healing ripples outward. When you start living with intention, the people around you feel it. They're reminded that redemption is real. That change is possible. That love can still win.

We live in a time where cynicism and division often dominate the headlines, but underneath all that noise is a deep hunger for connection, kindness, and truth. You don't have to save the whole world to make a difference; you just have to show up in yours. Be someone's reason to keep trying. Defend the people who can't defend themselves. Speak up when it's uncomfortable. Give when it's inconvenient. That's where true character is built, and that's how real change begins: one decision, one act of compassion, one life touched at a time. Legacy isn't just what you leave behind; it's what you build while you're still here. Let your comeback be someone else's blueprint.

Let your pain be fuel for purpose. If you've been blessed with a second chance, use it to lift others up. Be the kind of person who brings light into rooms, who restores hope to the hopeless, who reminds people what goodness looks like. In the end, it's not the trophies or titles that define us. It's the love we give, the truth we tell, and the lives we help rebuild. That's what lasts. That's what matters.

If there's one thing I've learned, it's that no matter how far you fall, you can always rise again—wiser, stronger, and more compassionate than before. The real victory isn't in never getting knocked down; it's in standing up with a renewed sense of purpose. My comeback wasn't just about reclaiming a career; it was about reclaiming gratitude, faith, and the chance to make a difference.

Over the years, I've seen the best and worst of what success can bring. I've seen how fame, money, and power can lift people up or pull them apart. What matters most isn't how high you climb, but how you treat people on the way up—and whether you're willing to reach back and help the next person climb, too. The truth is, life doesn't always go according to plan. You can lose everything—your title, your reputation, even your confidence—and still come out better on the other side if you hold on to integrity, humility, and faith. That's the lesson I hope my story shares: that a comeback isn't about erasing the past; it's about learning from it, owning it, and using it to build something stronger.

In life, as in sports, it's not about the scoreboard—it's about the impact you leave on people and the integrity with which you play the game. If your word still means something, if your heart still leads your choices, and if you can walk away knowing you made life a little better for someone else, that's the real win. Thank you for letting me share my story with you. Learning the lessons of resilience means we can all come together to light candles rather than curse the darkness.

About the Editor

Lavaille Lavette is a best-selling publisher, author, editor, and creative executive whose career bridges publishing, film, finance, and social entrepreneurship. As Managing Partner at Joyful Pen, One Street Studios, Lavette Books, JVL Media, and Orisha Capital Group, she continues to shape the global creative landscape across the U.S. and Africa. Her editorial work includes Finding Me by Viola Davis and Shut Up and Listen! by Tilman Fertitta—both New York Times best sellers—and The Gumbo Coalition by Marc Morial. As an author, Lavaille created The Adventures of Roopster Roux and the Jayylen Little Golden Book series, both in film and TV development. She is also the co-owner of The Roux, the world's first literacy-driven convenience store and gas station chain, bringing books and reading corners into everyday community spaces.

About the Author

Leigh Steinberg is a legendary sports agent, entrepreneur, and philanthropist whose career spans more than five decades. As Chairman of Leigh Steinberg Sports and Entertainment, he has represented over 300 professional athletes across multiple major sports, including eight NFL number-one overall draft picks, sixty-four first-round draft picks, and twelve Hall of Famers. He has negotiated more than $4 billion in contracts and helped direct over $1.2 billion toward charitable causes. Widely recognized as the real-life inspiration for Jerry Maguire, Leigh is one of the most influential voices in modern sports, known for elevating athlete advocacy, leadership, and social responsibility. His pioneering work in brain health led to the establishment of the Leigh Steinberg Foundation for Concussion, Traumatic Brain Injury, and Brain Health—advancing research, awareness, prevention, and long-term care solutions for athletes and communities worldwide.